Unterrichtsmodell

Series Editor: Hans Kröger

Utopia and Dystopia
Exploring Alternative Worlds

by Hauke Hoffmann,
Jonas Mücke and Andrea Steen

Schöningh

EINFACH ENGLISCH

Einzelarbeit
Partnerarbeit
Gruppenarbeit
Unterrichtsgespräch
Schreibauftrag
Hausaufgabe
filmische Präsentation
Projekt, offene Aufgabe
kreative Aufgabe
szenisches Spiel, Rollenspiel

Vorwort

Der Titel der Reihe **EinFach Englisch** verdeutlicht Zielsetzung und Programm zugleich. Einerseits soll Schülerinnen und Schülern auf einfache Art und Weise der Zugang zu klassischen, aber auch neuen literarischen Werken und Filmen ermöglicht werden, andererseits sollen Lehrerinnen und Lehrern in der Praxis erprobte Unterrichtsmodelle angeboten werden, die die wichtigsten methodisch-didaktischen Ansätze des Faches Englisch abdecken. Dabei sind die Modelle direkt, ohne langes Einlesen einsetzbar und stellen Unterrichtsarbeit konkret vor. Als besonders hilfreich für die Praxis haben sich dabei folgende Aspekte erwiesen, die für die Gestaltung der Reihe wesentlich sind:

- Überblick über **Figurenkonstellation**, ggf. **Filmszenen** und **Inhalt**
- **Klausuren** mit **Erwartungshorizont**
- **Arbeitsblätter**, **Tafelbilder** und **Leitfragen** für den Unterricht
- **Piktogramme** als Hinweise auf **Unterrichts-** und **Arbeitsformen**

Das Prinzip der **„Components"** ermöglicht darüber hinaus den variablen Einsatz der Modelle in unterschiedlich konzipierten Unterrichtsreihen. Dabei stehen Machbarkeit und Praxisnähe stets im Vordergrund.

Das vorliegende Modell bezieht sich auf folgende Textausgabe: *Utopia and Dystopia – Exploring Alternative Worlds*, Paderborn: Schöningh Verlag 2006, ISBN 978-3-14-041202-5

Sprachliche Betreuung: Simone Duxbury-Ziemer

Fotos: Cover: „Himmelsstürmer" – Skywalker, Skulptur von Jonathan Borofsky für die Documenta 9, Kassel 1992, © picture-alliance/HB Verlag; **S. 3:** © Cinetext Bildarchiv

www.schoeningh-schulbuch.de
Schöningh Verlag, Jühenplatz 1–3, 33098 Paderborn

Druck 5 4 3 2 / Jahr 2011 10 09 08
Die letzte Zahl bezeichnet das Jahr dieses Druckes.

Umschlaggestaltung: Peter Wypior; Bad Driburg
Druck und Bindung: AZ Druck und Datentechnik GmbH/Kempten (Allgäu)

ISBN 978-3-14-041204-9

Getting started

Look up the word "Armageddon" in an encyclopedia such as www.wikipedia.com or www.britannica.com and answer the following questions.

1. Where does the word come from and what does it stand for?
2. How do religious cults such as Jehovas Witnesses or the Rastafari Movement interpret it?
3. Find out what Jerry Bruckheimer's and Michael Bay's 1999 film *Armageddon,* starring Bruce Willis, Ben Affleck, Billy Bob Thornton and Liv Tyler, is about.

Then discuss the following topic in groups. Be prepared to share your results with your fellow students.

4. What will life on Earth be like in a hundred years from now?

Utopia and Dystopia – Exploring Alternative Worlds

Component 3: The modern classics: Dystopia – nightmare worlds 34

Component 4: The present 52

Component 5: Utopia or dystopia in poetry and song 79

Vorüberlegungen zum Einsatz der Textausgabe im Unterricht

Nachdem wir uns entschieden hatten, das Angebot des Verlages anzunehmen, eine Sammlung von Texten mit dem Titel *Utopia and Dystopia* zu erstellen, wurde uns sehr schnell klar, dass ein Hauptproblem nicht darin bestehen würde, passende Texte zu finden, sondern vielmehr zu entscheiden, was bei der schier unendlichen Anzahl von geeigneten Titeln verzichtbar erschien. Wir hoffen sehr, dass die vorliegende Mischung aus Bekanntem und Unbekanntem, Klassischem und Modernem gefällt und Schülerinnen und Schülern viel Stoff für spannende Lektüre und interessante Diskussionen liefert.
Wir sehen die Auszüge natürlich in erster Linie als Operationsobjekte für den Unterricht an, daneben aber auch als „Appetithäppchen", die den einen oder die andere neugierig machen, zum Lesen der Ganzschrift animieren und ggf. in einem Referat darüber berichten lassen sollen. Die gewählten Texte spannen einen Bogen, der fast 3000 Jahre Kulturgeschichte umfasst. Die Prophetenbücher (der erste Text ist ein Auszug aus dem Buch Jesaja) gehören zu den ältesten Teilen der Bibel. Der Koran entstand zwar erst ca. eineinhalb Jahrtausende später, wird hier aber aufgrund des inhaltlichen Zusammenhanges mit dem Jesaja-Text zusammen behandelt. Da auch die griechische Antike in Form zweier Exzerpte aus Platons *Republik* vertreten ist, kann zu Recht gesagt werden, dass die beiden Pfeiler abendländischer Kultur Berücksichtigung gefunden haben. Es folgen mit den Texten von Thomas More und Tommaso Campanella Auszüge aus zwei klassischen Utopien, die in Swifts *Gulliver's Travels* ihre satirische Antwort finden. Der *dritte Component* ist ganz den drei berühmtesten Dystopien des 19. und 20. Jahrhunderts gewidmet: Wells' *Time Machine,* Huxleys *Brave New World* und Orwells *1984.* Einen weiteren Schwerpunkt stellt dann im *vierten Component* die Gegenwartsliteratur dar, wobei hier nicht nur Prosa, sondern auch ein Auszug aus dem Drehbuch zu einem der populärsten Filme der letzten Jahrzehnte, *Matrix*, ausgewählt wurde. Im *letzten Component* soll dann kurz die Rolle, die utopische und dystopische Themen in der populären Musik spielen, untersucht werden. Ein kurzer Shakespeare-Text wird die Einheit beschließen.

Thematisch werden u. a. folgende Aspekte mehrfach angesprochen:

- Erziehung, Schule und Bildung
- Sex und das Verhältnis der Geschlechter zueinander
- Worauf beruht Glücklichsein?
- Das Verhältnis von individueller Freiheit und der Stabilität des Gemeinwesens
- Staatliche Unterdrückungsmechanismen
- Chancen und Gefahren der Gentechnologie
- Von Menschen verursachte globale Katastrophen

Hier sehen wir auch vielfältige Möglichkeiten für Facharbeiten und andere besondere Lernleistungen. Konkrete Themen könnten z. B. sein:

- Concepts of school and education in Plato's *Republic* and More's *Utopia*
- Opportunities and risks associated with genetic engineering
- Man-made global catastrophes
- *Brave New World* – a truly prophetic work of fiction?
- *Oryx and Crake* – fact and fiction
- Looking back: Orwell's *1984* and the Soviet Union under Stalin

- Looking back: George Orwell's *1984* and the Soviet Union under Stalin
- The chances and risks of American patriotism
- The new right movement – new evangelism in the US

Die Textsammlung eignet sich für Grund- und Leistungskurse der gymnasialen Oberstufe. Wenn alle Texte behandelt werden, gehen wir von einer Unterrichtszeit von 35 bis 40 Stunden aus.

Musterantworten zu den *while-reading questions* der Textausgabe befinden sich am Ende dieses Unterrichtsmodells (Anhang b, S. 85 ff.).

Klausuren

Im Folgenden werden zwei Klausurvorschläge vorgestellt.

Klausur 1 ist ein Auszug aus dem vierten „klassischen" dystopischen Roman des 20. Jahrhunderts, Ray Bradburys *Fahrenheit 451*. Zur Bearbeitung der Aufgaben sollten die Schülerinnen und Schüler mit Kapitel III. der Textsammlung (ggf. mit Ausnahme von *Time Machine)* vertraut sein.

Der Text zur **Klausur 2** ist der Schluss einer Kurzgeschichte von John D. MacDonald.
Da die dritte Aufgabe die Kenntnis des *Matrix*-Exzerpts voraussetzt, empfiehlt sich diese Klausur erst nach der Lektüre von Kapitel IV.

Beide Klausuren sind vom Schwierigkeitsgrad und der Länge der Textvorlage her grundsätzlich für Leistungs- und Grundkurse geeignet. Unterschiede zwischen Leistungs- und Grundkursfach zeigen sich im unterschiedlichen Niveau der Sprachverwendung, der Komplexität der verwendeten Techniken (z. B. beim Zusammenfassen, Interpretieren, Argumentieren, Kommentieren, Werten, kreativen Schreiben) und dem Maß an Sicherheit und Eigenständigkeit ihrer Anwendung.

Ray Bradbury, *Fahrenheit 451* (1953)

(The following extract is taken from chapter 3 of the novel.)

In this futuristic Californian society being a firefighter is a highly-regarded profession which is also pursued by Guy Monday. But instead of fighting fires, the firefighters of the future start fires themselves in houses in which they find books. One night, feeling exhausted and disillusioned with his job, Monday returns home. Still shaken by the night's events when he watched an old woman setting fire to herself, her home and her books, Monday starts to question the purpose and legitimacy of his profession. In this excerpt, Captain Beatty, his supervisor and friend, explains how and why the job profile has come to change.

[...] "Now let's take up the minorities in our civilization, shall we? Bigger the population, the more minorities. Don't step on the toes of the dog-lovers, the cat-lovers, doctors, lawyers, merchants, chiefs, Mormons, Baptists, Unitarians, second-generation Chinese, Swedes, Italians, Germans, Texans, Brooklynites, Irishmen, people from Oregon or Mexico. The people in this book, this play, this TV serial are not meant to represent any actual painters, cartographers, mechanics anywhere. The bigger your market, Montag, the less you handle controversy, remember that! All the minor minorities with their ears to be kept clean. Authors, full of evil thoughts, lock up your typewriters. They *did*. Magazines became a nice blend of vanilla tapioca. Books, so the snobbish critics said, were dishwater. No *wonder* books stopped selling, the critics said. But the public, knowing what it wanted [...], let the comic-books survive. And the three-dimensional sex-magazines, of course. There you have it, Montag. It didn't come from the Government down. There was no dictum, no declaration, no censorship, to start with, no!
Technology, mass exploitation, and minority pressure carried the trick. Today, thanks to them, you can stay happy all the time, you are allowed to read comics, the good old confessions, or trade-journals."
"Yes, but what about the firemen, then?" asked Montag.
"Ah." Beatty leaned forward in the faint mist of smoke from his pipe. "What more easily explained and natural? With school turning out more runners, jumpers, racers, tinkerers, grabbers, snatchers, fliers, and swimmers instead of examiners, critics, knowers, and imaginative creators, the word 'intellectual', of course, became the swear word it deserved to be. [...] Surely you remember the boy in your own school class who was exceptionally 'bright,' did most of the reciting and answering while the others sat like so many leaden idols, hating him. And wasn't it this bright boy you selected for beatings and tortures after hours? Of course it was. We must all be alike. Not everyone born free and equal, as the Constitution says, but everyone made equal. Each man the image of every other; then all are happy, for there are no mountains to make them cower, to judge themselves against. So! A book is a loaded gun in the house next door. Burn it. Take the shot from the weapon. Breach man's mind. Who knows who might be the target of the well-read man? Me? I won't stomach them for a minute. And so when houses were finally fire-proofed completely, all over the world [...] there was no longer need of firemen for the old purposes. They were given the new job, as custodians of our peace of mind, the focus of our understandable and rightful dread of being inferior; official censors, judges, and executors [...] You must understand that our civilization is so vast so that we can't have our minorities upset and stirred. Ask yourself, What do we want in this country, above all? People want to be happy, isn't that right? Haven't you heard it all your life? I want to be happy, people say. Well, aren't they? Don't we keep them moving, don't we give them fun? That's all we live for, isn't it? For pleasure, for titillation? And you must admit our culture provides plenty of these. [...]

(648 words, incl. introduction)

to step on the toes of here: to irritate, disturb

Brooklynite author-coined term: person from Brooklyn

tapioca substance used to thicken puddings etc.

tinkerer worker doing repairs

grabber unpleasant person who tries to touch sb in a sexual way

snatcher thief, (pl) thieves

to recite to repeat out loud

to cower *sich ducken*

to breach man's mind here: get control over people's thoughts

custodian caretaker

titillation excitement

Assignments

1. Summarize Beatty's main theses in your own words.
2. Compare Bradbury's futuristic society with those you read about in other dystopian excerpts dealt with in class (e.g. the Oceania of George Orwell's *1984*, the futuristic London of Aldous Huxley's *Brave New World*) and point out similarities between them.
3. Do you agree with the concepts of happiness, perfection and efficiency established by Beatty and state officials in the other texts (e.g. the Director of the Ministry of Truth or the Director of the Central London Hatchery)? Choose one of the characters and write either a **letter** to him **or** make up **a dialogue** in which you state your personal views and respond to the character's arguments. You may choose one of the quotes below as the starting point of your dialogue (letter), which should also show that you have some specific knowledge of the ideals and principles of the society you are referring to.

   "People want to be happy, isn't that right? Haven't you heard it all your life? I want to be happy, people say. Well, aren't they? Don't we keep them moving, don't we give them fun? That's all we live for, isn't it?" (Captain Beatty, Fahrenheit 451)

   "And that (here: the process of conditioning) is the secret of happiness and virtue – liking what you've got to do. All conditioning aims at that, making people like their inescapable social destiny." (The Director of the Central London Hatchery, Brave New World)

Erwartungshorizont zu Klausur 1

zu 1: Being the mastermind of state censorship, Captain Beatty gives a short historical outline of the development of mass entertainment and the disappearance of philosophy. Beatty continues by defending the moral aims of the ideal of censorship. He claims that equality can only be achieved through laws and government regulations as it is not given through birth. Beatty, moreover, explains that with their texts, authors usually offend people who belong to a different ethnicity, social class or who are less educated. They do not give clear simple answers but contradict each other. He complains that the contents of serious books trouble people and increase the divide between those who are well-read and those who are not. The Captain stresses that in the course of history it was the people themselves who abandoned serious literature, not the government. Beatty is convinced that under the current regulations, people are better off than they were before. Thus, firefighters have to prevent any changes to the status quo and, therefore, destroy those who do not agree with the regime's notion of happiness.

zu 2: All characters live in totalitarian repressive states; residents are unable to escape the "eyes" of the state; different institutions are employed to keep dissenters under control, e.g. Big Brother & the Ministry of Truth (*1984*), the firemen (*Fahrenheit 451*); disagreement and disloyalty are unwanted and eliminated; liberal principles are distorted; togetherness and harmony are considered evil and a threat to the state and are, therefore, not tolerated; individuality and diversity are seen as evil; regimes make use of propaganda (slogans, banners, Newspeak, book bans) and technological advances (e.g. telescreen, Bokanovsky Process) to increase control and repressive measures over residents and sway public opinion; language is distorted; the truth is powerfully provided by state officials – regimes pretend to protect their citizens when, in fact, they seek their own advantages; people are provided with mass entertainment and, thereby, deliberately kept ignorant; technological improvements are used to keep people in bondage; residents are vulnerable

zu 3: A dialogue between the Director of the Central London Hatchery (CLH) and a student (S).

CLH: And that (here: the process of conditioning) is the secret of happiness and virtue – liking what you've got to do. All conditioning aims at that, making people like their inescapable social destiny.

S: I don't think anybody should be given the right to determine somebody's fate. It's up to nature – not the government – to decide if someone is bright or less bright or good with his hands or well-read.

CLH: That is the past! You are probably too young to understand this. Technological advances have enabled us to produce the number of people we really need to maintain stability. What good are too many scholars, too many people who can repair cars or too many people who strive for power and positions in the government? We need workers (Epsilons) more than anything. We don't need them to think, we need them to get their jobs in the production done. And I'm sure that we can intensify the production of Epsilons, and that way, beat our rival labs overseas.

S: I believe that all human beings should benefit from technological improvements but they should not be used to perfect different means of indoctrination and terror used by the government against its citizens.

CLH: Well, you don't seem to get the point. Society would be too heterogeneous by now if we hadn't introduced the Bokanovsky process. We need standard men and women who have the same skills and the same intelligence. Otherwise, tensions would destabilize this country and civil wars might erupt.

S: Your idea of stability is really frightening.

CLH: You seem to forget that our new technologies have not only enabled us to increase the production of human beings, they also have helped us fight and ultimately eliminate fatal diseases. By closely watching the test tubes, we can prevent any abnormalities. We can produce perfect bodies. Wouldn't you like that?

S: Well, I have to disagree with you there too. While we should certainly use new technologies to treat diseases like cancer or AIDS, we should not try to define what perfection is or what a perfectly-shaped body looks like. I guess my idea of a perfect body is totally different from yours. I also think humans have to cope with diseases, otherwise they become vulnerable and weak.

John D. MacDonald: *Spectator Sport* (1950)

[...]

The subterranean corridor had once been used for underground trains. But with the reduction in population it had ceased to pay its way and had been taken over by World Senseways to house the sixty-five thousand Perms.

Dr. Rufus Maddon was taken, in his new shambling walk, to the shining cubicle. His name and the date of installation were written on a card and inserted in the door slot. Handriss stood enviously aside and watched the process.

The bored technicians worked rapidly. They stripped the unprotesting Rufus Maddon, took him inside his cubicle, forced him down onto the foam couch. They rolled him over onto his side, made the usual incision at the back of his neck, carefully slit the main motor nerves, leaving the senses, the heart and lungs intact. They checked the air conditioning and plugged him into the feeding schedule for that bank of Perms. Next they swung the handrods and footplates into position, gave him injections of local anesthetic, expertly flayed the palms of his hands and the soles of his feet, painted the raw flesh with the sticky nerve graft and held his hands closed around the rods, his feet against the plates until they adhered in the proper position.

Handriss glanced at his watch.

"Guess that's all we can watch, Al. Come along."

The two men walked back down the long corridor. Handriss said, "The lucky so and so. We have to work for it. I get my Perm in another year – right down here beside him. In the meantime we'll have to content ourselves with the band sets, holding onto those blasted knobs that don't let enough through to hardly raise the hair on the back of your neck."

Al sighed enviously. "Nothing to do for as long as he lives except twenty-four hours a day of being the hero of the most adventurous and glamorous and exciting stories that the race has been able to devise. No memories. I told them to dial him in on the Cowboy series. There's seven years of that now. It'll be more familiar to him. I'm electing Crime and Detection. Eleven years of that now, you know."

Roger Handriss chuckled and jabbed Al with his elbow. "Be smart, Al. Pick the Harem series."

Back in the cubicle the technicians were making the final adjustments. They inserted the sound buttons in Rufus Maddon's ears, deftly removed his eyelids, moved his head into just the right position and then pulled down the deeply concave shining screen so that Rufus Maddon's staring eyes looked directly into it.

The elder technician pulled the wall switch. He bent and peered into the screen. "Color okay, three dimensions okay. Come on, Joe, we got another to do before quitting."

They left, closed the metal door, locked it.

Inside the cubicle Dr. Rufus Maddon was riding slowly down the steep trail from the mesa to the cattle town on the plains. He was trail-weary and sun-blackened. There was an old score to settle. Feeney was about to foreclose on. Mary Ann's spread and Buck Hoskie, Mary Ann's crooked foreman, had threatened to shoot on sight.

Rufus Maddon wiped the sweat from his forehead on the back of a lean hard brown hero's band.

(541 words)

shambling shuffling, walking clumsily
cubicle small, cell-like room
incision cut
to slit here: to sever, cut
schedule timetable, plan
handrod grip, handle
to flay to remove the skin from
graft *Transplantat*
blasted knobs *etwa: verdammte/dämliche Griffe*
to devise to invent
to jab to punch
deft skillful
mesa flat topped hill as often seen in westerns
an old score to settle *etwa: eine alte Rechnung zu begleichen*
to foreclose on to confiscate
spread here: piece of land
crooked here: dishonest

Assignments

1. Sum up what happens to Rufus Maddon in this extract.
2. Would you say this is more a utopian or a dystopian short story? Give reasons for your opinion.
3. Choose one of the following assignments:
   a) Compare and contrast the "Perms" in MacDonald's story with the Matrix.
   b) If you could have your own "Perm", what would it be like? Write a letter to a friend of yours, telling him/her about it.

Erwartungshorizont zu Klausur 2

zu 1: Maddon is taken into a small cell, undressed, put on some kind of bed. His main motor nerves are severed, yet his circulation, senses, heart and lungs, etc. left intact. His hands and legs are positioned on rods and plates and the envious technicians make sure that he will be fed automatically. They finally position his head in front of a three-dimensional screen and let the reader know that from now on Maddon will not have to work any more, but will be able to enjoy his Perm for at least seven exciting years. In front of the screen, he will believe himself to be in the film as a cowboy hero fighting crime in the Wild West.

zu 2: Most students are expected to consider this story dystopian. They might argue that Maddon will not live a real life, but only play a role in a cliché-loaded movie. The removal of his eyelids will condemn him to a never-ending consumer role without sleep, rest or relaxation. On the other hand, the prospect of living an exciting life without work will probably be attractive to some of the students. The immense popularity of video games, in which players slip into the roles of superheroes might be considered, too.
They might also mention that Maddon, unlike the two technicians, has not chosen the Perm he is connected to himself (ll. 26f.). His walk is called "shambling" (l. 5), so he might have been drugged. He is "unprotesting" (l. 8), but has to be "forced ... down" (l. 9).

zu 3 a): During their first meeting, Morpheus explains to Leo that the Matrix "is the world that has been pulled over your eyes to blind you from the truth." This, of course, is similar to the Perm. The main difference comes out clearly if one considers Morpheus' following statement: "Like everyone else, you were born into bondage, kept inside a prison that you cannot smell, taste, or touch. A prison for your mind." So while the Perm is an escape route, some kind of eternal holiday for deserving or wealthy-enough persons, the Matrix has been developed for the ultimate exploitation of mankind.
On a technological level the Matrix and the Perms are very much alike: Human beings are kept in small boxes and plugged to different wires. They remain in these boxes until they die while the illusions of artificial worlds are projected onto them. Yet whereas the Perms are created through a three-dimensional screen and headphones, the Matrix is directly implemented into the human brain.

zu 3 b): The students are expected to use typical elements of an informal letter. For this part of the assignment, colloquial language is appropriate. Any further anticipation of what they will write about is hardly possible.

Konzeption des Unterrichtsmodells

Das vorliegende Unterrichtsmodell bietet Klausurvorschläge, Arbeitsblätter, Kopiervorlagen und methodische Anleitungen zu literaturwissenschaftlichen und inhaltlichen Aspekten der Textsammlung *Utopia and Dystopia – Exploring Alternative Worlds*. Des Weiteren finden Sie eine Vielzahl kreativer und handlungsorientierter Aufgaben in variierenden Arbeitsformen. Ziel ist eine möglichst intensive Auseinandersetzung der Schülerinnen und Schüler mit den Texten, bei welcher der Spaß an Literatur und kreativem Schreiben nicht zu kurz kommen soll.
Im Anhang finden Sie eine Liste von Gemälden zum Thema Apokalypse sowie Musterantworten für die *while-reading*-Fragen der Textsammlung (S. 84 ff.).

Die einzelnen *Components* folgen im Wesentlichen der Chronologie der Entstehung der Texte. Es ist aber durchaus möglich, die Reihenfolge der Behandlung der Exzerpte zu verändern, z. B. nach thematischen Aspekten, wie *genetic engineering* (Texte 2.2, 3.2, 4.3, 4.4 und 4.5) oder *perfect education* (Texte 1.4, 2.2, 2.3, 3.2 und 4.5). Auch das Weglassen einzelner Bausteine dürfte zu keinen größeren Verständnisproblemen führen.

Die meisten Texte sind für alle Lerngruppen der Qualifikationsphase der Sekundarstufe II geeignet. Lediglich den ersten Platon-Text (1.3) und den Auszug aus *Gulliver's Travels* (2.3) empfehlen wir wegen der sprachlichen Schwierigkeiten vorrangig zur Behandlung in Leistungskursen.

Component 1 soll – in aller Kürze – einen Eindruck von den beiden voneinander unabhängigen abendländischen Wurzeln utopischen Gedankengutes geben: religiösen prophetischen Büchern einerseits (hier vertreten durch Jesaja und Mohammed) und der griechischen Antike andererseits (in diesem Fall zwei Auszüge aus Platons *The Republic)*.
In ***Component 2*** kommen dann zunächst mit Thomas More und Tommaso Campanella zwei der wichtigsten Schriftsteller der Renaissance zu Wort und beschreiben, wie ihrer Meinung nach ideale Gesellschaften aussehen sollten. Der sich anschließende Text Jonathan Swifts ironisiert und karikiert als perfekt betrachtete Systeme und leitet insofern zu ***Component 3*** über, der ganz den drei klassischen Dystopien des 19./20. Jahrhunderts gewidmet ist: Wells' *Time Machine*, Huxleys *Brave New World* und Orwells *1984*. Der Übergang zu ***Component 4***, der sich ebenfalls ausschließlich mit alptraumhaften Welten/Gesellschaften beschäftigt, verläuft dann fließend: Hier werden Exzerpte von vier unserer Meinung nach wichtigen und interessanten Dystopien der letzten zwei Jahrzehnte sowie eine Kurzgeschichte und ein Auszug aus dem Drehbuch zu *Matrix* bearbeitet. Der abschließende ***Component 5*** untersucht dann noch kurz die Rolle von Utopien und Dystopien in der Popmusik und in einem Gedicht Shakespeares.

Zum Einstieg sollte das auch in der Textausgabe abgedruckte Gemälde *Triptych of The Last Judgement* von Hieronymus Bosch (ca. 1450–1516) betrachtet werden. Falls Ihr Fachbereich Kunst ein Dia oder eine Folie dieses berühmten Bildes hat, sollte selbiges zusätzlich an die Wand geworfen werden. Noch einfacher wäre die Bildbetrachtung, wenn Sie über einen Beamer mit Internetanschluss verfügten. Damit könnten Sie auch Ausschnitte dieses detailreichen Meisterwerkes perfekt vergrößern. Sie finden das Gemälde – wie fast alle Hauptwerke europäischer Malerei vom 12. bis 19. Jahrhundert – in bestechender Qualität unter http://www.wga.hu/[1]

Lassen Sie Ihre Schülerinnen und Schüler in Gruppen die folgenden Fragen aus der Textausgabe beantworten:

1. According to Bosch, what will happen on Judgement Day?

   Jesus has returned to Earth to decide on the fate of all mankind (both the living and the dead). A few pious souls are elected to live eternally in heaven (top left), whereas the vast majority are condemned to horrifying tortures in Hell. Obviously, Bosch is far more interested in the fate of the sinners than in the ever-lasting happiness of the righteous. Some of the deadly sins (and the dreadful fate of those who committed them) can be recognized: The avaricious are being boiled in the great cauldron just visible beneath one of the buildings in the central panel. A fat man is being forced to drink from a barrel held by two devils; his "refreshment" comes from a demon squatting in the window above. The lecherous woman on the roof will soon be raped by a lizard-like monster already slithering across her loins, while being serenaded by two other demons. On the cliffs to the right, devilish blacksmiths are hammering other victims on anvils – one is actually being shod like a horse; these unfortunate souls are guilty of the sin of anger.

2. What might the damned in the painting have done to deserve their fate?

   They must have sinned against God.

3. You probably have an idea of the alternative, too. What will be the destiny of the blessed? Give details.

   They will live "happily ever after" in the proximity of God. They probably won't have to work for their nourishment in a peaceful land of milk and honey (like Adam and Eve before the Fall). Everything they need or wish to have will be given to them as a reward for their pious earthly lives.

4. As you can see, Bosch loved to go into details in this painting, too. For him and his contemporaries, "hell" was considered to be the most horrible place imaginable, which people were afraid of all their lives, whereas "heaven" was an ideal everybody tried to reach. What would be "heaven" or "hell" for you? You can either draw a picture or write a short text.

   (The students' personal "lands of milk and honey" are, of course, very difficult to anticipate and very much dependent on their special tastes and preferences, as are their individual nightmare societies. Nevertheless, this is worthwhile preparatory work for the components to come, during which the pupils will be confronted with other people's utopias and dystopias.)

---

1 Auf dieser Webseite finden Sie auch eine Interpretation des Bildes. OH-Folien desselben können dort ebenfalls bestellt werden.

Besonders die Ergebnisse der letzten Aufgabe sollten ausführlich in den Gruppen und im Plenum dargestellt und ggf. diskutiert werden. Fordern Sie Ihre Schülerinnen und Schüler auf, ihre Aufzeichnungen aufzubewahren und später mit dem zu vergleichen, was gelesen worden ist. Es wird sicherlich interessante Parallelen geben.

Die Besprechung dieses Bildes ist ein idealer Einstieg in die Diskussion der ersten beiden Texte der Sammlung, dem in Teilen utopischen, in Teilen dystopischen Auszug aus dem Buch Jesajas und dem Koran.

Component 1

The beginnings

Das erste Kapitel der Textausgabe behandelt in aller Kürze die „Urformen" von Utopie und Dystopie, die in den heiligen Schriften von Christen, Juden und Moslems einerseits und der klassischen griechischen Philosophie andererseits zu finden sind. Gedanken der Propheten Jesaja und Mohammed, wie auch Ideen Platons, werden in späteren Kapiteln in ähnlicher Form wieder auftauchen.

1.1 Beat swords into plowshares: *Book of Isaiah*, 2, 2–4; 11, 6–8; 35, 5–9

Die klassischen Propheten des Alten Testaments – mit Ausnahme von Jonas und Habakuk – verkünden alle zweierlei: Sie prophezeien zunächst Unheil für die Israeliten, da diese die Gebote des Herrn missachten, und trösten dann das Volk in Krisenzeit und Verbannung, indem sie ihm Heil für die Zukunft verkünden.
So handelt auch der erste Teil des Buches Jesaja (wissenschaftliche Bezeichnung: Protojesaja) von Strafen, die dem Volk Israel aufgrund seiner Sünden angekündigt werden. Die letzten Kapitel des Buches (Deuterojesaja), denen der dritte Textauszug entnommen wurde, sind später, in einer völlig veränderten historischen Situation entstanden. In der Zwischenzeit ist Jerusalem zerstört und die israelitische Oberschicht ins babylonische Exil verschleppt worden. Aufgabe des Propheten ist es nun, das helfende und rettende Eingreifen Gottes anzukündigen.
Wir schlagen vor, die Jesaja-Texte aufgrund der inhaltliche Nähe zusammen mit jenen aus dem Koran zu behandeln.

1.2 Fruits piled one above another and virgin-pure Companions: *The Qur'an*, Suren 2, 25; 47, 15; 56, 1–44

Auch Mohammed prophezeit sowohl Heil als auch Unheil. Im Gegensatz zum Buch Jesaja gibt es hier aber keine zeitliche Entwicklung. Mohammed wendet sich an ein und dieselbe Generation von Mitmenschen und verkündigt den Gerechten Gottes ewigwährenden Lohn, den Ungerechten nie endende Qualen. Die Beschreibung des paradiesischen Lebens ist äußerst detailliert. Auffällig ist die häufige Wiederholung vom glücklichen Leben in einem friedvollen, blühenden, fruchtbaren Garten, der Rückschlüsse auf die Lebensbedingungen der damaligen Bewohner Arabiens zulässt.

Für die Behandlung der auf die Zukunft gerichteten Gedanken der beiden Propheten schlagen wir folgendes Verfahren vor:
Sie teilen Ihre Lerngruppe zunächst in zwei (möglichst) gleich große Gruppen ein, z. B. mithilfe von Spielkarten: Wer eine rote Karte zieht, gehört zur Gruppe A, wer eine schwarze

zieht, zur Gruppe B. Schülerinnen und Schüler der ersten Gruppe beschäftigen sich zunächst in Stillarbeit (ca. 20 Minuten) mit den Jesaja-Texten, die zweite Gruppe mit denen aus dem Koran. Dazu erhalten sie jeweils *Copy 1 oder 2* und die Aufgabe, sich intensiv mit ihrem jeweiligen Text vertraut zu machen, da sie später als „Experten" Fragen der anderen Gruppen beantworten werden müssen. Nachdem die Aufgaben auf den Arbeitsblättern bearbeitet worden sind, bilden die Schülerinnen und Schüler zwei Stuhlkreise, der innere Kreis (Gruppe A) blickt nach außen, der äußere (Gruppe B) nach innen, sodass sich immer jeweils zwei Schülerinnen oder Schüler gegenübersitzen. Zunächst befragen dann Mitglieder der Gruppe A ihrer Aufgabenstellung entsprechend ihre Partner (ca. 4 Minuten lang) und tragen die Ergebnisse auf ihrem Blatt unten ein. Anschließend geben Sie das Kommando zum ersten „Partnerwechsel", z. B.: *„Inner circle clockwise two".* Das würde bedeuten, dass die Mitglieder der Gruppe A – im Uhrzeigersinn – zwei Plätze weiter nach rechts rücken. Auch Oberstufenschülern macht ein derartiger Gesprächspartnerwechsel unserer Erfahrung nach immer Spaß, besonders, wenn Schülerinnen oder Schüler die Kommandos falsch verstehen und z. B. statt *„clockwise" „anti-clockwise"* unterwegs sind.
In dieser zweiten Runde müssen die Mitglieder der Gruppe A dann ihren neuen Partnern aus der Gruppe B erzählen, was sie über die Korantexte erfahren haben (ca. 3 Minuten lang). Ist etwas nicht richtig oder unvollständig, werden sie von ihren neuen Partnern korrigiert. Auf diese Weise wird sichergestellt, dass nichts Falsches gelernt wird. (Um ganz sicher zu gehen, können Sie natürlich am Ende der Stunde auch noch einmal im Plenum die „Jesaja-Experten" über den Koran und die „Koran-Experten" über Jesaja referieren und/oder die Ergebnisse an die Tafel schreiben lassen; als notwendig hat sich dieses allerdings in unseren Versuchen nicht erwiesen.)
In der dritten Runde, nachdem wieder neue Partner gesucht worden sind (z. B. mithilfe des Kommandos *„outer circle anti-clockwise three")*, befragen jetzt die Koranexperten, also die Mitglieder der Gruppe B, mithilfe ihrer Arbeitsblätter ihre Gegenüber zu Jesaja. In der vierten und letzten Runde überprüfen sie dann ihre Erkenntnisse wie oben beschrieben mit wieder anderen Mitschülern.
Die Vorteile dieses Verfahrens liegen auf der Hand: Der Sprechanteil der Schülerinnen und Schüler ist sehr hoch. Durch den mehrfachen Austausch des Gelernten verfestigt sich dieses in einem viel höheren Maße, als das durch bloßes Lesen und die Bearbeitung eines Arbeitsblattes geschehen kann. Man kommt durch die arbeitsteilige Bearbeitung der beiden Texte zügig voran. Und nicht zuletzt: Den Schülerinnen und Schülern macht dieses Verfahren in der Regel viel Spaß, gerade zu Beginn einer Reihe ein nicht zu überschätzender Vorteil!

Zur Vertiefung und Festigung empfehlen wir folgende schriftliche Hausaufgabe:

1. These texts were first written in the Middle East, a landscape dominated by vast deserts. If an Inuit in the Arctic were to describe paradise, what might he write?

   The Inuit would probably dream of a (slightly) warmer climate with food in abundance.

2. Obviously a person's image of paradise is influenced by his/her living conditions. Explain the connection.

   Whatever people are missing in their lives seems to become an object of desire for them. If they cannot achieve it during their lifetime, they hope to gain it after their death.

Lösungsvorschläge zu *Copy 1 (Isaiah):*

1. See biographical assumptions on p. 8: priest for 58 years (ca. 739 – 686 B. C.); considered himself a "spokesman of God"; announced first punishment and later the liberation of the chosen people.
2. They will gather at "the Lord's house" on the "mountain of the Lord" to be taught by him and "walk in his paths".
3. Weapons will be melted down and made into tools.
4. They will all be herbivores and live together peacefully.
5. All their disabilities will be healed.
6. The desert will be turned into green land.

Lösungsvorschläge zu *Copy 2* (*Qur'an*):

1. See biographical aspects on p. 9: prophet of the Islam (569 – 632 A. D.) to whom the Qur'an was disclosed.
2. The rivers will either be full of eternally clean water or milk that does not turn sour, delicious wine, honey and fruit.
3. There will be earthquakes and the total annihilation of mountains.
4. The "Foremost in Faith", the most pious believers, will be closest to Allah. Together with the "Companions of the Right hand" they will enjoy all kinds of fresh and fine-tasting food and drink (including wine that will neither make them drunk nor cause a hangover). The "Companions of the Right Hand" will also be given beautiful virgins of their own age.
5. The "Companions of the Left Hand" will have to suffer in fire and boiling water for all eternity.

Additional discussion results:

1. Isaiah: desert, dangerous animals, war, particularly hard life for disabled people
2. Qur'an: desert, lack of food and water, obviously many of his contemporaries did not live very pious lives in Muhammad's eyes

Group A: Isaiah

Read your texts carefully and take notes. You will later have to inform other students about them. They will ask for information about

1. Isaiah's life and prophecies ______

2. what many people will do "in the last days" ______

3. the future of weapons and war ______

4. the relationship between herbivores (plant-eating animals), carnivores (meat-eating animals) and children, as well as their future eating habits ______

5. the future fate of physically-disabled people ______

6. changes in the countryside ______

If there is time left, briefly discuss what these texts reveal about the living conditions of Isaiah and his contemporaries.
Later you will have to gather information about the Qur'an and its prophet, Muhammad. Ask your partner about

1. Muhammad's life and how the Qur'an came into existence ______

2. what kind of rivers are promised to the righteous (people who are honest, just, moral) ______

3. which destructions in nature will be caused by the "Event inevitable" ______

4. who the "Foremost in Faith" and the "Companions of the Right Hand" are and what their fate will be like ______

5. who the "Companions of the Left Hand" are and what their future will look like ______

Group B: The Qur'an

Read your texts carefully and take notes. You will later have to inform other students about them. They will ask for information about

1. Muhammad's life and how the Qur'an came into existence ______

______

2. what kind of rivers are promised to the righteous (people who are honest, just, moral) ______

______

3. which destructions in nature will be caused by the "Event inevitable" ______

______

4. who the "Foremost in Faith" and the "Companions of the Right Hand" are and what their fate will be like

______

5. who the "Companions of the Left Hand" are and what their future will look like ______

______

If there is time left, briefly discuss what these texts reveal about the living conditions in Arabia in Muhammad's time.
Later you will have to gather information about one of the most important prophets of the Old Testament. Ask your partner about

1. Isaiah's life and prophecies ______

______

2. what many people will do "in the last days" ______

______

3. the future of weapons and war ______

______

4. the relationship between herbivores (plant-eating animals), carnivores (meat-eating animals) and children, as well as their future eating habits ______

______

5. the future fate of physically-disabled people ______

______

6. changes in the countryside ______

______

1.3 The greatest happiness of the whole: Plato, *The Republic*, book 3

Der erste Platon-Text ist unseres Erachtens recht schwierig und darum vor allem für Leistungskurse oder philosophisch vorgebildete Schülerinnen und Schüler zu empfehlen. Den zweiten kann man hingegen ohne Bedenken auch mit einem Grundkurs ohne Vorkenntnisse erarbeiten.
Zur sokratischen Methode können Sie unter http://en.wikipedia.org/wiki/Socrates weitere Informationen finden.

Wir empfehlen, den Text zunächst still lesen zu lassen. Anschließend sind in möglichst leistungshomogenen Gruppen alle *while-reading questions* und die folgenden Aufgaben in ca. 30 Minuten zu bearbeiten. Die Ergebnisse sollten anschließend arbeitsteilig an die Tafel geschrieben, verglichen und diskutiert werden.

1. p. 12, ll. 21 – 27: Think of another example of personal happiness that would negatively affect the happiness of the whole community.

E.g. a cook who spends the whole day in his master's wine cellar; a soldier who is allowed to spend most of his time eating and drinking and who is not fit enough to do his job properly in times of emergency

2. Would you like to live in Kallipolis? Why/why not?

We expect most students to answer in the negative. They will probably consider it positive that no poverty exists in Kallipolis, yet they will not accept the impossibility of accumulating worldly possessions.

3. "Der Einzelne ist nichts, das Volk ist alles" was preached from German pulpits and by German nationalists from the last decades of the 19th century to the end of World War II. Even today, right-wing extremists make use of this attitude. Is this an idea of Plato's? What were the consequences of such thinking during the Third Reich?

The thought goes far beyond Plato's ideas. The Greek philosopher warned that too much personal wealth might cause the leaders to neglect their duties. He never called into question their right to live. People sacrificed their lives by the millions.

4. What is the main difference between Plato's idea of true happiness and the ideals you found in Isaiah and the Qur'an?

The main difference is, of course, that Plato's ideal society is to be created by people themselves whereas the religious writings expect God to intervene and create a new paradise.

1.4 Sacred marriages: Plato, *The Republic*

Als Hausaufgabe empfiehlt sich der zweite, einfachere Platon-Text. Lassen Sie Ihre Schülerinnen und Schüler die *while-reading questions* schriftlich beantworten (Lösungen s. S. 85 f.) und erteilen Sie zusätzlich folgenden Auftrag:

Visit the web pages http://www.shoa.de/content/view/183/41 and http://www.jewishvirtuallibrary.org/jsource/Holocaust/Lebensborn.html. Compare and contrast Himmler's Lebensborn project and Plato's idea of an ideal marriage arrangement.

Da die erste Webseite auf Deutsch verfasst wurde, kann diese Hausaufgabe auch als Übung für die in einer zunehmenden Anzahl von Bundesländern abiturrelevante Mediationsaufgabe angesehen werden.

Lösungsvorschläge:

According to Plato, it is ridiculous to carefully choose ideal mates when breeding animals, yet leave the choice of human sex partners to chance or emotions, since their offspring will decide on the future of the community. He explains that the elite of the human race must therefore only be allowed to copulate amongst themselves to create superior human beings, who will become the future leaders. The "inferior" men and women should either have no sex at all, or their offspring (as well as children of the elite born handicapped) should be killed. "Brides" and "grooms" are to be brought together during special events.
In addition to that, there are supposed to be faked lotteries with the help of which men of the elite will earn the right to have sex with as many women as possible and in this way, sire as many children as possible (out of wedlock). These children will be taken away from their mothers to be raised in accordance with the state's needs.
Himmler and the "Lebensborn" project pursued a very similar aim: the creation of future "Herrenmenschen". In order to create a "super-race", tall and blue-eyed women of unquestionable "Arian" heritage were brought together with members of the SS in order to be made pregnant by them. In the "Lebensborn" homes, they could later give birth under comparatively luxurious and safe conditions. Most of the children were not raised by their mothers, but stayed in the homes to be educated there or were adopted by SS families.
In later years, when more and more future soldiers were needed, children in occupied territories, who looked "Arian", were abducted and also raised in the "Lebensborn" homes. The major parallel is obvious: the selection of elite partners to create ideal offspring. The elimination of "worthless" children, which we find in the Plato text, was, of course, also practiced by the Nazis, though this is not mentioned on the two web pages. Moreover, the children of the elite are, in both cases, not raised and educated by their parents but by government authorities.
Plato's weird lottery and the abduction of seemingly "Arian" children by the Nazis do not find an equivalent in the other text(s).

Component 2

The classics: Utopia – life as it should be

2.1 Till death do us part: Thomas More, *Utopia*

Thomas Mores Buch erschließt sich einem heutigen Leser nur noch als Produkt seiner Zeit. Galt *Utopia* vielen seiner Zeitgenossen als politisch revolutionär, ungemein liberal und tolerant, wären für die meisten von uns die strengen Regeln und Gesetze Utopias heute doch alles andere als erstrebenswert. Auch die im Text genannten Hochzeits- und Scheidungsregularien erscheinen uns heute im besten Fall naiv (z. B. die nackte Präsentation von Bräutigam und Braut), im schlimmeren Fall spießig und intolerant (kein vorehelicher Sex, Scheidung auch bei Einigung der Partner kaum möglich).
Versteht man Mores Buch jedoch als konstruktive Kritik an Missständen seiner Zeit, wird *Utopia* zu einer hochinteressanten historischen Quelle.
Die Kopiervorlage zu Heirats- und Scheidungsbräuchen vom Mittelalter bis zur Reformation *(Copy 3)* soll den Schülerinnen und Schülern helfen, dieses zu erkennen. Macht der Text doch klar, dass More hier nicht die übermäßige Strenge, sondern vielmehr die sittliche Laxheit seiner Zeitgenossen kritisiert, indem er die Utopier als viel moralischer und enthaltsamer als seine Mitmenschen darstellt.
Nach Besprechung der Hausaufgabe (Lebensborn-Projekt), die thematisch auf den More-Text vorbereitet, sollte dieser zunächst still zur Kenntnis genommen und die *while-reading questions* beantwortet werden. Nach Sammlung der Ergebnisse an der Tafel kann der Text von *Copy 3* vorgelesen werden. Dieser Text soll den Schülerinnen und Schülern u. a. klarmachen, dass zweifellos nicht jeder Leser mit Thomas More übereinstimmte, sondern viele seine teilweise modernen, teilweise aber auch puritanischen Empfehlungen als Zumutungen oder Einschränkungen empfanden.

Lösungsvorschläge zu *Copy 3*:

1. Without doubt, the betrothal was the more important part. The first ever Christian wedding ceremony in England did not take place until the middle of the 10th century.
   Up till the 16th century, marriage was widely considered to be a purely worldly matter.
2. They regarded marriage and divorce as something secular which was to be performed by worldly authorities, not the Church. Milton even recommended "self-divorce".

Im Folgenden können in Form einer vereinfachten *Debate* mithilfe von *Copy 4* Argumente für und gegen Mores Ideale ausgetauscht werden.
Nach Austeilen der Kopiervorlage machen Sie Ihren Schülerinnen und Schülern unbedingt klar, dass bei dieser in angelsächsischen Ländern besonders an Schulen und Universitäten weit verbreiteten intellektuellen Wettkampfform die Teilnehmerinnen und Teilnehmer durchaus auch Meinungen vertreten, die nicht ihre eigenen sind. Gerade die Unterstützer von Mores Position werden überwiegend gegen eigene Überzeugungen reden müssen.
Die Schülerinnen und Schüler sollten sich in Gruppen von drei bis vier Teilnehmerinnen oder

Marriage and divorce from the Middle Ages to the time of the Reformation

It is a little-known fact that in 950 A.D. a Christian priest blessed a couple during a wedding ceremony for the very first time in England, according to a Saxon prayer book, the so-called "Ritual of Durham". Before that – and it remained so well into the 16th century – marriage had been a purely worldly matter. People let themselves in for in two important stages: the betrothal, the couple's mutual pledge of fidelity, and the actual wedding ceremony, which normally took place considerably later. The "spousal" (= betrothal) was considered to be the more important part. It consisted of the exchange of consent and the first sexual intercourse. In other words: Sex began at the moment of engagement and not on the wedding day.

Children born to couples who were conceived after betrothal were regarded as legitimate as soon as the parents married. Therefore, it might be said that a wedding in church was often mainly triggered by pregnancy or childbirth.

Despite the entry in the above-mentioned "Ritual of Durham", it was not until the middle of the 16th century that betrothal and wedding ceremony were joined. Up to then, sexual relationships and a life under the same roof had been permitted immediately after an engagement.

The Reformation never regarded marriage as a sacrament, i.e. a holy ritual act instituted by Jesus himself like baptism or the Eucharist. Martin Luther called it "a worldly affair ... that is the responsibility of the government" and not the Church. Just like Luther, the Puritans treated marriage as something secular, thus the ceremony was not to be performed by a minister, but by a Justice of the Peace".

Whereas the Catholic Church considered marriage to be indissoluble except by death, most Protestant reformers did not think so at all. The English poet John Milton (1608 – 1674), a Puritan writer best known for his epic poems "Paradise Lost" (1667) and "Paradise Regained" (1671), even advocated self-divorce without any involvement of church or government. When love was missing, marriage, in his eyes, was mere sinful pretence that should be ended as soon as possible.

betrothal *Verlobung*
pledge promise, vow

the Eucharist Christian sacrament commemorating Jesus' and his disciples' last supper on the night before his crucifixion, the so-called Maundy Thursday.
secular worldly, not spiritual or religious
Justice of the Peace (JP) judge in the lowest courts of law
indissoluble *unauflösbar*

1. What was considered to be more important in medieval England, the betrothal or the Christian wedding ceremony? How do you know?
2. What did Luther and other Reformers think of marriage and divorce?

Debating

A debate is a formalized discussion between two sides with strict rules:
a) The proposition must defend the motion by giving arguments for it, the opposition must attack the motion by giving arguments against it.
b) The order of the speakers is: first speaker for the proposition (arguments for) → first speaker of the opposition (arguments against) → second speaker of the proposition (s.a.) → second speaker of the opposition (s.a.) → third speaker of the proposition (rebuts main points of the opposition) → third speaker of the opposition (rebuts main points of the proposition). Debaters give coherent speeches on the basis of just a few notes. It's important that they successfully engage their audience.
The speaking time is limited, in international tournaments to eight minutes, in school to four.

the proposition the debater(s) in favour of a thesis
motion here: proposal
the opposition the debater(s) against the thesis
to rebut to contradict, refute

Ladies and gentlemen,
the proposition believes that …
Now, first and foremost, …
Second, …
And last, but not least, …

Ladies and gentlemen,
the opposition would like to cast some reasonable doubt on the above case.
Our scepticism revolves around a few basic questions:
The proposition assumes …
Yet we fear that …
Second, …

Ladies and gentlemen,
the proposition can assure you that …
Ladies and gentlemen, what have we shown you? That it works, that it can be done, so let the motion stand.

Ladies and gentlemen,
the opposition is still far from convinced.
Let us just take a look at …
Another problem: …
We therefore beg to oppose the motion.

Ladies and gentlemen,
the proposition has certainly considered all the implications very carefully before proposing this motion. …

Ladies and gentlemen, …

Teilnehmern auf die Debatte vorbereiten. Die Gruppen sammeln Argumente (nicht nur die in den Texten genannten) und wählen jeweils einen *speaker* (ca. 15 Minuten). Die jeweiligen Sprecherinnen und Sprecher, die eine Meinung teilen, stimmen anschließend kurz ihre Strategie ab und vermeiden damit möglichst unnötige Wiederholungen (ca. 10 Minuten). Dann wird – wie in *Copy 4* geschildert – abwechselnd argumentiert (hier sollte die Redezeit auf maximal zwei Minuten pro Sprecherin oder Sprecher begrenzt werden). Alle anderen Schülerinnen und Schüler hören aufmerksam zu und beobachten, ggf. mit einem einfachen Bewertungsbogen, wie die Vortragenden sich geben. Kriterien wie Einsatz der Stimme, Körpersprache, Überzeugungskraft, Augenkontakt und Aufeinandereingehen sollten dabei eine mindestens genauso wichtige Rolle spielen wie die sprachliche Kompetenz. Diese Bewertungsmaßstäbe können von den „Nichtrednern" in der Zeit, in der diese sich in den oben geschilderten Pro- und Kontra-More-Gruppen treffen, selbst festgelegt werden.
Bei der Überschaubarkeit des Themas denken wir, dass je zwei, maximal drei Redner pro oder kontra More ausreichen. Wichtig ist danach die Auswertung durch die gesamte Lerngruppe.

Die zu diskutierende These könnte lauten:

The marriage and divorce laws of the Utopians should be adopted by our present-day society.

Possible argumentation:

1. Pros

- no unwanted pregnancies
- no young teen pregnancies
- no polygamy, ergo: no AIDS or other sexually-transmitted diseases
- a means against an unwanted and/or unlimited population increase
- strong position of family and family values
- long abstention from sex teaches young men and women to control their desires and will later help them to remain faithful to their spouses
- the method of choosing one' s partner is not ridiculous, but rather shows an approving attitude towards sex since "good qualities" [in a partner] are not enough (p. 16, ll. 10–19)
- the fact that divorces are very rare gives financial security to women
- security in the case of old age and disease is guaranteed (p. 17, ll. 32f.)
- separation "by mutual consent" (p. 17, ll. 33–36) is possible
- "True Love Waits"[1]

2. Cons

- unnatural and unnecessary suppression of one's sexual desires
- sex has always been an important part of (young) people's lives, "True Love Can**not** Wait"
- unrepentant offenders, who had premarital sex, and adulterers will never be allowed to marry (again), i.e. have sex – this is inhumane and unnatural

[1] Vielleicht haben Ihre Schülerinnen und Schüler bereits von dieser in den USA und mittlerweile auch in Deutschland weit verbreiteten Bewegung gehört, die „Revolutionary Purity" gelobt und für die Sex vor und außerhalb der Ehe tabu ist. Weitere Informationen finden Sie hier: http://www.lifeway.com/tlw/

- far higher risk of men becoming rapists if they are not allowed to live out their sexuality in any legal way
- punishment of the families of young offenders is unfair and inhumane
- being presented to one's future partner in the nude by an older person is embarrassing and disgraceful
- More was not progressive, but reactionary – considering marriage and divorce customs before him and at his time
- Even some other Puritans took a far more liberal view (e.g. John Milton)

Als Hausaufgabe empfiehlt sich die Lektüre des nächsten Textes, in Kombination mit der schriftlichen Beantwortung der *while-reading-questions.*

2.2 The coupling of males and females: Tommaso Campanella, *The City of the Sun*

Die Bedeutung, die Thomas Mores *Utopia* für die europäischen Intellektuellen seiner Zeit hatte, wird den Schülerinnen und Schülern schnell klar, wenn sie anfangen, Campanella zu lesen. Nicht nur die Form, sondern auch der Inhalt seines bekanntesten Buches lehnt sich klar an More an. Allerdings scheint Campanella die Schwächen seiner Zeitgenossen besser zu verstehen, da er allzu harsche Normen der Gesellschaft Utopias spürbar abschwächt, z. B. durch Herabsetzen des Mindestalters von Männern, das zum Sex berechtigt, und die Erkenntnis, das sexuelle Bedürfnisse nicht einfach durch Verbote unterdrückt werden können (vgl. S. 18, Z. 11–13). Doch auch den Schülerinnen und Schülern bereits bekanntes platonisches Denken ist bei Campanella leicht aufzuspüren, z. B. die Kriterien, nach denen Sexualpartner füreinander ausgesucht werden, und Platons Ideen zur Vermeidung von Eifersucht (S. 19, Z. 29–32).
Während der erste Teil des Textes also vor allem an Bekanntes anschließt, bereitet der zweite Teil auf ein Thema vor, das in mehreren noch folgenden Texten (z. B. von Swift und Anderson) im Mittelpunkt stehen wird: die ideale Erziehung und Bildung junger Menschen.
Da das Beantworten der *while-reading questions,* die Teil der Hausaufgabe waren, in der Regel keine größeren Schwierigkeiten bereitet, muss die Ergebnissicherung nicht im Plenum, sondern kann zur Abwechslung auch in Gruppen geschehen. Zusätzlich würden wir die Gruppen die folgenden Fragen und Aufgaben gemeinsam bearbeiten lassen (Gruppenarbeitsphase ca. 20 Minuten):

1. Where does the influence of Plato show clearly?

   p. 18, ll. 4–8: "breeding … and coupling of males and females"
   p. 19, ll. 29–35: Plato's thoughts are mentioned but rejected since "in the City of the Sun there is no need to cheat so as to match ugly men with ugly women, for there are no ugly ones among them"

2. Where do we find ideas that are familiar from Thomas More's "Utopia"?

3. To what extent does Campanella seem to be more realistic than More?

The book is also mainly narrated by a traveller who has visited a far away island with ideal conditions.
p. 18, ll. 11 – 13 are very similar to More, yet Campanella seems to be more realistic as, on his island, sexual intercourse is – under special circumstances – also allowed between younger people.

4. Briefly sum up a typical life story of a boy or girl born to this utopian society. Write the first person singular form as if this were a report on your own life.

for two years cared for by my mother – then put into the care of teachers of my own sex – studies of the alphabet and art – also learnt to walk, run, and wrestle – wore colourful clothing – from age seven taught sciences and later "mechanical arts" – less talented became farmers, more talented like me allowed to live and work in the city – a lot of physical exercise – platonic love possible, but sexual intercourse only with partners selected by authorities

Nach Vergleich der Ergebnisse im Plenum empfehlen wir, mit den Schülerinnen und Schülern in den Computerraum zu gehen. (Alternativ kann die folgende Aufgabe natürlich auch daheim erledigt werden).

The American billionaire Tom Monaghan, founder of Domino's Pizza (pizza chain located in over 60 countries worldwide) and former owner of the Detroit Tigers (US Major League baseball team), has recently started to build his Catholic utopia, a new university town in Southwest Florida, reminiscent of Campanella's *City of the Sun*. More about his so-called *Ave Maria Project* here: http://www.avemaria.com/ and here: http://www.tagesschau.de/ausland/avemaria10.html

What, in Monaghan's eyes, will make *Ave Maria* such a special place? Prepare a short oral statement. Include why you would or would not like to be a student there.

- a mix-use walking town, a reflection of traditional European town centres with street level boutiques and an authentic diversity of restaurants and cafes
- living and learning will form an integrated whole
- beautiful and safe environment, where neighbours will care about each other
- Ave Maria University, AMU: an institution with high standards of academic excellence
- AMU, a centre of educational, intellectual and spiritual activities, plans to grow to approximately 6,000 undergraduate and graduate students
- lots of recreational facilities
- devotion to preserving the town's environmental resources
- alternative to other Catholic schools, which according to Monaghan are failing on key issues like religious observance, sexual behaviour and opposition to abortion
- single-sex dorms only, a quarter of the classes taught by orthodox priests, students urged to become priests and nuns
- pharmacies not allowed to sell condoms or dispense contraceptives

- private chapels within walking distance of each home
- Mass said hourly, seven days a week

Lassen Sie anschließend Ihre Schülerinnen und Schüler Paare bilden und sich gegenseitig ihr Kurzreferat vortragen. Ermutigen Sie vorher zur gegenseitigen Kritik, auch was Körpersprache, Augenkontakt, Intonation etc. angeht. Dabei sollten natürlich nicht nur Schwächen, sondern gerade auch Stärken des Vortrages Erwähnung finden.
Sicher fällt den Schülerinnen und Schülern der Unterschied in der Selbst- und Fremddarstellung auf. Ganz nebenbei üben sie mithilfe des „Tagesschau"-Textes auch die bereits auf S. 27 erwähnte abitur-relevante Mediationsaufgabe.

Lassen Sie Ihre Schülerinnen und Schüler daheim den folgenden Text von Jonathan Swift vorbereiten. Weisen Sie sie darauf hin, dass aufgrund sprachlicher Schwierigkeiten ein zumindest zweimaliges Lesen unabdingbar ist. Beim zweiten Mal sollten auch die *while-reading questions* schriftlich beantwortet werden.

2.3 Perfected education: Jonathan Swift, *Gulliver's Travels*

Wie der erste Text Platons ist der vorliegende Auszug aus *Gulliver's Travels* aufgrund der erhöhten Schwierigkeit besonders für Leistungskurse zu empfehlen.

Das Thema „Ideal education", mit dem sich bereits der vorhergehende Ausschnitt beschäftigte, wird hier fortgesetzt. Allerdings könnten die Intentionen der beiden Autoren nicht unterschiedlicher sein: Während Campanella eine seiner Meinung nach ideale Gesellschaft beschreibt, nutzt Swift die Waffen des Satirikers, um auf realexistierende Missstände hinzuweisen bzw. seiner Wut auf die Partei der *Whigs*, die sich notwendiger Hilfe für die von englischer Ausbeutung geplagte arme katholische Bevölkerungsmehrheit Irlands beständig verweigerte, Luft zu machen.[1]
Wie Campanella war auch Swift von Thomas Mores *Utopia* beeindruckt und nennt ihn im Buch III von *Gulliver's Travels* einen der sechs größten Verteidiger der Freiheit aller Zeiten (zusammen u. a. mit Sokrates, Cato und Brutus). Auch die Form des *Gulliver* ähnelt der von Mores und Campanellas Büchern sehr.
Im ersten Teil des Romans, der Gullivers Besuch auf der Insel Lilliput zum Inhalt hat, gibt es einerseits Passagen, in denen Swift eindeutig das England seiner Zeit karikiert, z. B. in den vielen absurden königlichen Proklamationen, im pompösen Verhalten der Beamten, in den unterschiedlichen Bildungsmöglichkeiten von Jungen und Mädchen oder in der end- und sinnlosen Diskussion zu dem Thema, ob ein Ei am dickeren oder schmaleren Ende aufzuschlagen sei. Andererseits gibt es Abschnitte, die utopische Ideale enthalten, die ähnlich wie bei More und Campanella Gegenwelten zur traurigen Realität aufzeigen wollen.
Diese beiden alternierenden Ansätze in Swifts Satire erklärt Ian Johnston vom Boston College so:
"If the strange new country is recognizably similar to the reader's own culture, then comic distortions in the new world enable the writer to satirize the familiar in a host of different ways, providing, in effect, a cartoon style view of the reader's own world.
If the strange new country is some sort of utopia – a perfectly realized vision of the ideals often proclaimed but generally violated in the reader's own world – then the satirist can manipulate the discrepancy between the ideal new world of the fiction and the corrupt

[1] Mehr zu Swift und der irischen Frage finden Sie hier: http://www.sparknotes.com/lit/modestproposal/context.html

world of the reader to illustrate repeatedly just how empty the pretensions to goodness really are in the reader's world."[1]
Diese beiden Sätze sollten den Schülerinnen und Schülern als Tafelanschrieb oder auf einer Folie zugänglich gemacht werden, damit diese selber zu einem Urteil darüber kommen können, welcher der beiden satirischen Ansätze in dem vorliegenden Exzerpt vor allem zum Tragen kommt.

Nach Besprechung der Hausaufgabe (Bearbeitung der *while-reading questions* zum Swift-Text) empfehlen wir, zunächst in einer Gruppenarbeitsphase die folgende Tabelle ausfüllen zu lassen. (Die dritte Spalte, die so in Johnstons Ansatz nicht vorkommt, bereitet auf die nächsten Kapitel der Textsammlung vor, in denen, wie bereits erwähnt, *Education* eine zentrale Rolle spielen wird. Der Swift-Text dient insofern auch als Übergang von der Utopie der Renaissance zur Dystopie der Neuzeit.)

Ironic distortions and other allusions to Swift's England	**Utopian ideals**	**Nightmarish thoughts**

Lösungsvorschläge zur Tabelle:

• human life: miserable (p. 20, l. 12) • unjust class distinctions (p. 21, l. 3f.) • children of nobles always busy (p. 21, ll. 18–21) • not allowed to talk to servants who would only teach them follies (p. 21, l. 25 + p. 22, ll. 5–10)	• general education for almost all children, skilled teachers take into consideration their origin, abilities and interests (p. 21, ll. 2–11) • school fees according to parents' income (p. 22, ll. 28–33) • at least basic education for all boys and girls (utopian thought in Swift's time) • free hospital treatment for everyone • beggars unknown	• parents not allowed to see their children alone or to show affection • cruel punishment for talkative chambermaids

Trotz der dritten Spalte gehen wir davon aus, dass die meisten Schülerinnen und Schüler den überwiegend utopischen Charakter dieses Exzerpts erkennen.
Zum Abschluss der Behandlung des zweiten Kapitels der Textausgabe sollten nun – falls dies noch nicht geschehen ist – die Gemeinsamkeiten und Unterschiede der drei Textauszüge herausgestellt werden (siehe Einleitungen zu Campanella und Swift auf den Seiten 18 und 20). Auch die Definitionen von Utopie und Dystopie im Anhang der Textausgabe können jetzt gelesen werden (S. 89f.).

[1] http://www.thomasmorestudies.org/curriculum/swift.html Hier finden Sie auch interessante Ausführungen zu Swifts Verhältnis zu Thomas More.

Component 3

The modern classics: Dystopia – nightmare worlds

3.1 The sunset of mankind: H. G. Wells, *The Time Machine*

Zusammen mit George Orwells *1984* und Aldous Huxley's *Brave New World* ist Wells' Roman Ausdruck des Technikpessimismus, der sich bereits am Ende des 19. Jahrhunderts unter Intellektuellen ausbreitet. Wells anfängliche Begeisterung für die Errungenschaften der Technik hält in seinen Texten nicht lange an. Fortan thematisiert er die Gefahren, die im menschlichen Streben nach Perfektion liegen, so auch ersichtlich im ausgewählten Auszug aus seinem Roman *The Time Machine.*

Am Anfang des Romans steht ein Wissenschaftler der Gegenwart (hier in England am Ende des 19. Jahrhunderts), der seinen Freunden eine Maschine vorstellt, mit der er sich in der Zeit bewegen kann. Nach seiner Rückkehr von einer solchen Zeitreise erzählt er seinen Freunden von seinen Erlebnissen und von den Schlussfolgerungen, die er vor allem in Bezug auf die Folgen der fortschreitenden Technisierung gezogen hat.

Der Textauszug, der das Ausgeliefertsein der schwachen wehrlosen *Eloi* gegenüber den in der Unterwelt lebenden *Morlock* thematisiert, ist nach unserer Erfahrung ein geeigneter Impuls, um vor allem technikinteressierte Schülerinnen und Schüler für eine Auseinandersetzung mit den Folgen der Technisierung der Gegenwart zu motivieren, insbesondere wenn es um die Grenzen (?) des Wirtschaftswachstums geht. Besonders dieser Textauszug ist auf sprachlicher Ebene für den Einsatz in Grundkursen geeignet.

Die Schülerinnen und Schüler werden, so wie der Zeitreisende, die *Eloi* anfangs um deren paradiesische Lebensumstände beneiden, aber auch schnell deren sorgenfreies Leben infrage stellen. Grundsätzlich schlagen wir die Erarbeitung des Auszugs in zwei Abschnitten vor und begeben uns somit wie der Protagonist des Romans auf eine Zeitreise.

Wir schlagen vor, dass die Schülerinnen und Schüler den ersten Teil des Auszugs (also bis S. 26, Z. 4) vorbereitend zu Hause lesen. Zur Unterstützung des Leseverständnisses erhalten sie Satzanfänge, die sie parallel oder nach dem Lesen beenden sollen *(Copy 5, obere Hälfte).*

Im Stundeneinstieg tauschen die Schülerinnen und Schüler in Partnerarbeit ihre Leseergebnisse aus. Fragen, die sich an dieser Stelle ergeben und in der Partnerarbeit nicht geklärt werden können, notieren die Schülerinnen und Schüler an der Tafel mit dem Ziel, zum Ende der Stunde eine Klärung herbeizuführen.

Lösungsvorschläge zu *Copy 5*:

1. that the world has changed considerably (introduction).
2. the Eloi, little people of the future, who are following him (p. 23, ll. 1 f.).
3. having the same soft hairless visage (p. 23, l. 3).
4. they are all identically dressed and share the same girlish plumpness (p. 23, ll. 3 ff.).
5. at ease and seemingly secure (p. 23, l. 13), yet also weak representatives of humanity upon the wane (p. 24, l. 42 – p. 25, l. 3).
6. have been overcome by evolution (p. 25, ll. 11–38).

7. the Eloi wear glorious clothes, live in splendid shelters, but never seem to waste time working. He calls this society a "social paradise" (p. 25, l. 41 – p. 26, l. 3).

Während die häusliche Leseaufgabe auf die Charakterisierung der oberirdisch lebenden *Eloi* abzielt, soll in dieser Stunde das Lebensumfeld dieser scheinbar sorgenfreien Kreaturen im Mittelpunkt stehen. Dafür erstellen die Schülerinnen und Schüler ein *visual mind map,* mithilfe dessen sie die Lebenswelt der *Eloi* vollständig beschreiben sollen. Dafür stellen sie sich das auf *Copy 5* (untere Hälfte) zu findende Szenario vor, das in ein Rollenspiel münden soll.
Der vorletzte Satz des 1. Leseabschnitts ("It was natural on that golden evening that I should jump at the idea of a social paradise", S. 26, Z. 1–3) reicht nach unserer Erfahrung am Stundenende als Impuls aus, um von den Schülerinnen und Schülern eine Zwischeneinschätzung darüber zu erhalten, ob die Welt der *Eloi* beneidenswert oder sogar erstrebenswert ist.
Im nächsten Unterrichtsabschnitt wird auf der inhaltlichen Ebene das *social paradise* der *Eloi* mit dem Dasein der *loathsome* und *ape-like Morlock* der *underworld* kontrastiert. Dahinter stehen für Wells natürlich die Konsequenzen des blinden Vertrauens der meisten Menschen in die Verheißungen der sich entwickelnden Industriegesellschaft. Der Autor (in der Person des Zeitreisenden) blickt von nun an pessimistisch in die Zukunft und konfrontiert den Leser im nächsten Reiseabschnitt mit den von ihm prognostizierten Wirkungen der Industrialisierung auf die Verfassung moderner Gesellschaften.
Bevor der nächste Abschnitt mit der Hilfe von Verständnisfragen von den Schülern inhaltlich erschlossen wird, schlagen wir die Methode des *interpretation questionnaire (Copy 6)* vor. Entweder können die folgenden Impulse eine vorbereitende Hausaufgabe sein oder im Stundeneinstieg arbeitsteilig (2 Fragen/Partner) bearbeitet und die Überlegungen *(guesses)* im Plenum genannt werden. Es handelt sich hierbei nicht um Aussagen, denen mit einfachen „Ja"/„Nein"-Antworten begegnet werden kann; die Leserinnen und Leser setzen sich mit den im ersten Textabschnitt implizierten Zweifeln des Zeitreisenden und seinen Erklärungsansätzen auseinander und kommen zu unterschiedlichen Interpretationen der Lebensumstände der *Eloi.* Nach der Lektüre des zweiten Abschnitts sind diese überprüfbar und münden nach unserer Erfahrung direkt in eine kontroverse Abschlussdiskussion über Wachstumsgrenzen und Technikglauben.

Lösungsvorschläge zu *Copy 6*:

1. The Eloi have run out of resources to maintain these buildings. Or: They do not care for the architecture of their ancestors. They are not interested in culture and history. Or: They have decided that one must not try to stop the decay of material things and interfere with the processes of nature.
2. They don't live in families, but in one large community.
3. In this paradise-like world of the future "the strength of a man and the softness of a woman" (p. 23, ll. 15 f.) are no longer needed.
4. Everything seems to belong to everybody. Has the idea of communism become reality? The Time Traveller himself speaks of a "social paradise" (p. 26, ll. 2f).
5. Evolution and selective breeding have perfected flora and fauna, which give the Eloi everything they need. (Here is a clear parallel to the conceptions of paradise in the texts from the Bible and the Qur'an.)
6. E.g. cholera, malaria (no gnats), tuberculosis, smallpox, AIDS, measles, mumps, chickenpox, ...
7. Does somebody else make these clothes for the Eloi?
8. See 5.

Reading comprehension

After travelling in time, the Time Traveller finds himself in the year 802,701.

1. He sees ______________________________

____

2. Soon he makes contact with ______________________________

____

3. He describes them as ______________________________

____

4. What strikes him as peculiar about men and women is that ______________________________

____

5. He considers them ______________________________

____

6. To the Time Traveller's surprise, fatal diseases ______________________________

____

7. The Time Traveller is amazed that ______________________________

____

The Eloi are overwhelmed by the Time Traveller's visit and, as they seem to show no fear towards strangers, they decide to take their visitor on a tour around their surroundings. The Eloi are a confident people and the Time Traveller gains the impression that they live a life of play and toilless abundance. They, therefore, proudly present their surroundings.
Together with a partner draw a visual mind map which contains the details of the Elois' physical surroundings and shows their luxurious life on the surface of the earth. Later use your mind map when you take the time traveller (i.e. your classmates) on a tour.

Passages in the excerpt which you should focus on to fulfill the task

- there are great palaces but most of them in ruins (p. 24, ll. 29–31)
- there are no hedges or signs of private property (p. 24, ll. 34 f.)
- the earth has become a garden (p. 24, ll. 35 f.)
- there are fruits and sweet and delightful flowers (everywhere) (p. 25, ll. 34 f.)
- brilliant butterflies are flying hither and thither (p. 25, ll. 35 f.)
- the Eloi are housed in splendid shelters (p. 25, ll. 41 f.)
- there are no factories, manufacturers or other places of work (p. 25, ll. 43 f.)
- there are no shops, traffic, advertising (p. 25, l. 44 – p. 26, l. 1)
- it is a golden evening (p. 26, ll. 1 f.)

Interpretation questionnaire

Try to give as many suggestions as possible with respect to the Time Traveller's theories in the first part of the excerpt.

1. Historical buildings are in an appalling state. What does the poor state of the buildings indicate?

2. There are no individual houses. In what groupings do the Eloi live together?

3. There are no visible differences between the sexes, and the texture and physical features of the Eloi are alike. Why?

4. There are no signs of private property. Why?

5. There is no sign of agriculture. The whole earth has become a garden. What do people live on? Why have the Eloi stopped cultivating the fields?

6. Diseases have been stamped out. What kind of diseases might people have combated successfully?

7. The Eloi are dressed admirably. How can they be so beautifully dressed even though nobody seems to work?

8. The Eloi are not engaged in labour. How can they, then, maintain their high standard of life?

Der Impuls für die Abschlussdiskussion könnte lauten:

Are technological advances positive or do people ultimately become feeble and vulnerable like the Eloi?

Zur Vertiefung und Weiterarbeit empfehlen wir den *BBC News* Text *"Human species 'may split in two'"*, der zeigt, dass Wells' Idee einer sich aufspaltenden Menschheit auch von Wissenschaftlern als möglich angesehen wird (http://news.bbc.co.uk/2/hi/uk_news/6057734.stm).

3.2 The secret of happiness and virtue: Aldous Huxley, *Brave New World*

Im Gegensatz zu George Orwell, der seine Hauptwerke *Animal Farm* und *1984* erst nach der historischen Erfahrung der Entstehung zweier totalitärer Regime und der Tragik des Zweiten Weltkriegs schrieb, waren es bei Huxley „Vorahnungen" vom Aufkommen repressiver politischer Systeme und die Entwicklung der Atombombe, die er in *Brave New World* verarbeitet hat. In seiner Vorstellung würde die Technisierung des menschlichen Lebens (insbesondere die Informations- und Gentechnologie) langfristig zu einem Konflikt zwischen den Freiheitsbedürfnissen des Individuums und den Machtvorstellungen politischer Systeme führen. In *Brave New World* dienen wissenschaftliche Fortschritte der Entwicklung immer rigiderer Kontrollinstanzen, die die Regierenden einsetzen, insbesondere um die demographische und moralische Entwicklung der Bevölkerung vollständig zu regulieren. Während sich die Staatsmacht in Orwells *1984* in Überwachung, Einschüchterung und innerem Terror auf der Grundlage technischer Neuerungen manifestiert, belässt Huxley die Bewohner des *World State* in Ignoranz und künstlicher Freude, Mittel der Repression werden nicht benötigt. Zweifel an der Illegitimität des politischen Systems werden damit ausgeschlossen.

Der ausgewählte Textauszug steht am Beginn des Romans und führt den Leser (und mit ihm zusammen eine Gruppe Studenten) in das *Central London Hatchery* des Jahres A.F. 632. Der Direktor präsentiert stolz die einzelnen Abteilungen seiner wissenschaftlichen Einrichtung, in der der Bedarf des *World State* an Humankapital gedeckt wird. Die Reproduktion auf natürlichem Wege ist nicht mehr vorgesehen. Die Studenten (die Leser) werden nun mit den verschiedenen Stationen und Prozessen der künstlichen Befruchtung vertraut gemacht.
Da es sich hierbei um einen sowohl inhaltlich als auch sprachlich anspruchsvollen Text handelt, sollte er am besten in Abschnitten erarbeitet werden. Er eignet sich besonders für den Einsatz in Leistungskursen, obwohl auf der naturwissenschaftlichen Ebene auch Kursteilnehmerinnen und Kursteilnehmer, die andere Leistungskurse belegt haben, oft gut über den aktuellen Stand in der Genforschung informiert sind.
Wir schlagen vor, dass die Schülerinnen und Schüler während der Bearbeitung dieses relativ umfangreichen Textauszugs einen *layout plan* anfertigen, der über die Ausmaße und die Logistik der *Central London Hatchery* Auskunft gibt. Ein solcher *layout plan* könnte am Ende der Erarbeitung einerseits nochmals helfen, das Leseverständnis der Schülerinnen und Schüler zu überprüfen, und kann andererseits auch die Grundlage für eine Abschlusswertung sein. Am Ende der inhaltlichen Erarbeitung des Textes wird so die Brutalität und Perversität der *Brave New World* nochmals anschaulich deutlich.
Der erste Vorschlag zum vorliegenden Auszug thematisiert die äußere Beschreibung der *Brave New World*, insbesondere den Aufbau und Zweck der *Central London Hatchery (CLH).* Um den Leseeinstieg zu erleichtern, schlagen wir vor, dass die Schülerinnen und Schüler zunächst auf der Grundlage von Begriffen (mit zusätzlichen Impulsfragen) aus der Textvorlage über den Handlungsrahmen des Romans spekulieren. Sie können die Begriffe individu-

ell oder auf Gruppen aufteilen (auch mehrfach, sodass eine größere Vielfalt an Ideen zusammengetragen wird). Diese Vermutungen werden nach der Lesephase (teilweise) bestätigt bzw. revidiert und in manchen Fällen lassen sie sich erst nach der Lektüre des gesamten Textauszugs vollständig einordnen. Nutzen Sie für den Leseeinstieg *Copy 7,* die geeignete Begriffe und Impulsfragen enthält.

Im Anschluss schlagen wir die Lektüre des ersten Textabschnitts vor (bis S. 29, Z. 16). Der Leseauftrag könnte einfach darin bestehen, die Vermutungen der Einstiegsphase zu überprüfen; es können aber auch zusätzlich folgende Verständnisfragen, auf die Sie in jedem Falle nach der Lektüre eingehen sollten, direkt an die Schülerinnen und Schüler weitergegeben werden:

1. What is the purpose of the Central London Hatchery and Conditioning Centre?
2. Who guides the students around the Centre and what is the guide's function?
3. The 'f' in "a.f." stands for Henry Ford, the car-maker (cf. "A.D." Anno Domini – in the year of the Lord). Why have the citizens of BNW made him their idol? What does Henry Ford stand for and how does he relate to the new world?

Der folgende Leseabschnitt (S. 29, Z. 17, bis S. 32, Z. 12) soll von den Schülern mithilfe der *while-reading questions* vorbereitend zu Hause gelesen werden. Je nach Leistungsfähigkeit Ihres Kurses kann der Text natürlich nun auch vollständig vorbereitend gelesen werden.

Am Stundenanfang steht die Überprüfung der Leseaufträge. Wir schlagen vor, dass in diesem Unterrichtsabschnitt zentrale Konzepte des *World State (Perfection, Efficiency, Stability, Progress),* die zweifellos in der gesellschaftlichen Rhetorik von jeher positiv besetzt und erst nach genauerer Überlegung ambivalent sind, einer vorläufigen Bewertung unterzogen werden. (Diese Begriffe sind natürlich für alle Texte der Textausgabe zentral; daher lassen sich hier gut Beispiele aus bereits bearbeiteten Materialien finden.) Für die Erarbeitung der begrifflichen Ambivalenz schlagen wir die sog. *chessboard activity* vor (vgl. S. 41). Diese Methode hat zum Ziel, die Schülerinnen und Schüler für die Ambivalenz der o.g. Begriffe zu sensibilisieren.

An der Tafel (oder auf einem Poster) bereiten Sie ein Schachmuster (mit nicht zu kleinen weißen und schwarzen Feldern) vor. Die weißen Felder stehen für positive Aspekte, die schwarzen für negative. Die Schülerinnen und Schüler erhalten Papierstreifen. Zu Beginn werden die Kursteilnehmerinnen und -teilnehmer gebeten, o.g. Begriffe auf dem Schachbrett begründend einzuordnen, zunächst textunabhängig wie im folgenden Beispiel. Sie heften die Begriffe nach dieser kurzen Plenumsphase an die gewünschte Stelle, also positive Begriffe auf ein weißes, negative auf ein schwarzes Feld. In unserer Unterrichtspraxis stießen die Schülerinnen und Schüler schon an dieser Stelle auf die Ambivalenz der Begriffe und ihren euphemistischen Charakter.

4. Is the concept of Perfection positive or negative?

   Perfection is always something positive. Just take the subject of health: Abnormalities should be eradicated so that people can use their full potential and do not have to rely on other people's help. On the other hand, Perfection reduces the diversity of human life. Nobody, moreover, has the right and the capability to define Perfection.

Phrases and expressions

The excerpt we are going to deal with in class draws our attention to a place called "The Central London Hatchery" – a kind of maternity ward of the future. What do the following phrases and expressions taken from the excerpt reveal about this place, its atmosphere and its purpose? What strikes you as peculiar or different from maternity wards of the present? Look up any unknown words.

- Embryo Store (What is its purpose? What is being stored and why?)
- Microscope (Why would one need a microscope in a maternity warden?)
- Fertilizing Room (What could its purpose be?)
- Polished tubes (What could the tubes be used for?)
- Pale-corpse-coloured rubber gloves (Who wears them and why?)
- Social Predestination Room (What could its purpose be?)
- Bottling Room (What could its purpose be?)
- Scarcely-breathing silence (What does this tell us about the work atmosphere?)
- Year of Stability (What could *stability* refer to? What other mottos can you think of or have you heard of?)
- Absentminded, soliloquizing hum (What does this tell us about the atmosphere at the CLH?)
- Conditioning Centre (What could the purpose of this room be?)
- Incubators (What are they needed for)?

Genauso gehen sie mit den Begriffen *Efficiency, Stability, Progress* vor.
Die Schülerinnen und Schüler sollen diese Begriffe nun auf deren Ambivalenz im *World State* prüfen, aussagekräftige Zitate (aus den Ausführungen und Erklärungen des Direktors) auf Papierstreifen notieren und anschließend auf dem Schachfeld entweder positiv oder negativ einordnen. Sie gehen arbeitsteilig vor, d.h. jede Gruppe beschäftigt sich mit einem der Begriffe und findet Beispiele im Text, die auf deren Verwendung (und Bedeutung) im *World State* schließen lassen. Da es sich z.T. um längere Zitate handelt, genügt es natürlich, wenn die Schülerinnen und Schüler Stichworte (mit Angabe der Zeilennummern) notieren. Sie präsentieren anschließend die Textstellen und ordnen sie auf dem *chessboard* ein. Doppelnennungen sind möglich.

Lösungsvorschlag für die *chessboard activity*:

Alternativ könnten auch die folgenden Zitate genannt werden:

Perfection: "Can you tell us the record for a single ovary, Mr. Foster? — Sixteen thousand and twelve in this Centre [...] Sixteen thousand and twelve; in one hundred and eighty-nine batches of identicals. But of course they've done much better..." (p. 31, ll. 38ff.)
Efficiency: "[how the eggs] were inspected for abnormalities, counted ... [spermatozoa] at a minimum concentration of one hundred thousand per cubic centimeter..." (p. 29, ll. 40ff.); "... if any of the eggs remained unfertilized, it was again immersed, and, if necessary, yet again..." (p. 30, ll. 2ff.); "... every bud will grow into a perfectly formed embryo, and every embryo into a full-sized adult. Making ninety-six human beings grow where only one grew before ..." (p. 30, ll. 12ff.); "... On a very slowly moving band a rack-full of test-tubes was entering a large metal

box, another rack-full was emerging. Machinery faintly purred ..." (p. 30, ll. 21 ff.); "Millions of identical twins. The principle of mass production at last applied to biology..." (p. 31, ll. 14 ff.); "Sixteen thousand and twelve; in one hundred and eighty-nine batches of identicals. But of course they've done much better..." (p. 31, l. 43 ff.)
Progress: "By which time the original egg was in a fair way to becoming anything from eight to ninety-six embryos – a prodigious improvement [...] on nature. Identical twins – but not in piddling twos and threes as in the old viviparous days, [...] actually by dozens, by scores at a time." (p. 30, l. 34 ff.) "Singapore has often produced over sixteen thousand five hundred; and Mombasa has actually touched the seventeen thousand mark [...] still, we mean to beat them if we can ..." (p. 32, ll. 1 ff.)
Stability: "Bokanovsky's Process is one of the major instruments of social stability [...] Standard men and women; in uniform batches. The whole of a small factory staffed with the products of a single bokanovskified egg." (p. 31, ll. 1 ff.); "[The problem of community, identity, stability] ... solved by standard Gammas, unvarying Deltas, uniform Epsilons..." (p. 31, ll. 13 ff.); "... For in nature it takes thirty years for two hundred eggs to reach maturity. But our business is to stabilize the population at this moment, here and now..." (p. 31, ll. 23 ff.)

Abschließend werden die Ideale der *Brave New World (Perfection, Efficiency, Stability, Progress)* bewertet. Es stellt sich heraus, dass es sich bei ihnen um Euphemismen handelt, die den Bewohnern in Huxleys Welt eine Unbeschwertheit bescheren sollen, die Kritik am politischen System unnötig und unmöglich macht. Verweisen Sie an dieser Stelle auf die Gegenwart und die Debatten um effizientes Wirtschaften, den uneingeschränkten Fortschrittsglauben, die Perfektionierung technischer Vorgänge oder menschlicher Körper und vertiefen Sie damit die Begriffsarbeit. Ordnen Sie die Begriffe abschließend nochmals auf dem *chessboard* ein:

Is people's longing for perfection positive (e.g. perfect looks)?
Can you think of contemporary technological advances which you consider negative?

Nach unserer Erfahrung ergeben sich an dieser Stelle interessante und schüleraktivierende Diskussionen im Plenum.
Wenn nicht schon im letzten Arbeitsschritt geschehen, sollte der letzte Textabschnitt (ab S. 32, Z. 13) wiederum vorbereitend gelesen werden. Offensichtlich ziehen weder die Angestellten der *CLH* noch die Besucher die Ausführungen des Direktors in Zweifel. Vorsichtige Zwischenfragen der Besucher rufen Unverständnis und Spott bei Mr. Foster hervor (z. B. S. 35, Z. 25 ff.). Das *CLH* steht mit anderen Forschungseinrichtungen im Wettbewerb – Singapur und Mombasa werden im Auszug genannt (S. 32, Z. 1 f.).
Um abschließend das Leseverständnis der Schülerinnen und Schüler zu überprüfen und gleichzeitig eine interpretatorische Leistung einzufordern (auch der *layout plan* könnte dafür herangezogen werden), könnte in Kleingruppenarbeit ein kurzer Anzeigentext oder eine Kampagne für das *CLH* entworfen werden, deren Präsentation noch in der selben Stunde (oder in der nächsten Stunde) erfolgt. Folgendes Szenario bietet sich dafür an:

Who is afraid of designer babies? The Central London Hatchery has run out of reliable scientists who are dedicated to the World State's motto of "Community, Identity, Stability". Most young academics start their career at research centres in Singapore or Mombasa as the laboratories there work more efficiently and have gained a remarkable reputation worldwide. The director hires you to start a publicity campaign or design a newspaper advert attracting young scholars who want to start their career at CLH. Point out the institution's accomplishments, its technological advances and the inspiring atmosphere young scholars would enjoy at the CLH.

Für eine Abschlussdiskussion sollten Sie auf die Gegenwartsrelevanz von Huxleys Text verweisen und könnten folgenden Impuls einsetzen:

To what extent does the director's explanation compare with the economic values of our society in which the individual's happiness derives from the satisfaction of their needs and progress is equated with growth and prosperity?

3.3 Freedom is slavery: George Orwell, *1984*

Mit *1984* stellt sich George Orwell in die Reihe englischer Autoren der ersten Hälfte des 20. Jahrhunderts, die vor den Folgen totalitärer politischer Systeme warnen, in denen der technische Fortschritt in der Informationstechnologie vor allem für die Perfektionierung repressiver Kontrollmechanismen verwendet wird.
Es ist das Jahr 1984. Im Textauszug werden die Schülerinnen und Schüler mit dem trostlosen Alltagsleben von Winston Smith – einem unbedeutenden Parteimitglied der Staatspartei Ozeaniens – bekannt gemacht. Der Textauszug liefert eine detaillierte Beschreibung des Wohn- und Arbeitsumfelds des Protagonisten. Besonders viel Raum nimmt dabei die Beschreibung des *Ministry of Truth* (in *Newspeak:* Minitrue), gleichzeitig Smiths Arbeitgeber, und dessen wichtigstem Machtinstrument – der *telescreen* – ein. Dem euphemistischen Gebrauch des Freiheitsbegriffs kommt dabei eine zentrale Bedeutung zu. Daher schlagen wir vor, dass die Schülerinnen und Schüler vor der ersten Lesephase in einem *writing storm* in 5 bis 10 Minuten folgende Fragen schriftlich beantworten.

What are the freedoms you enjoy? Which freedoms are denied to you?

Sie sollen dabei ihre spontanen Gedanken zu den Fragen aufschreiben und anschließend im Plenum vortragen. Mithilfe dieser Methode erhalten vor allem leistungsschwache Kursteilnehmerinnen und -teilnehmer die Möglichkeit, zunächst Gedanken zu formulieren, um sie dann mit größerer Sicherheit im Plenum vorzutragen.
Es hat sich als günstig erwiesen, den Beginn des Auszugs (bis S. 39, Z. 15) noch in derselben Stunde gemeinsam im Unterricht zu lesen, um erste Eindrücke über den Protagonisten und seine Lebenswirklichkeit zu gewinnen, wodurch die eigenständige Lektüre des übrigen Texts erleichtert wird. Wir schlagen vor, dass die Schülerinnen und Schüler dabei zunächst arbeitsteilig Notizen oder Zitate zu folgenden Aspekten anfertigen:

Describe

1. the protagonist,
2. the inside of the apartment block,
3. the outside of the apartment block,
4. the design and function of the telescreen.

Die Gruppenergebnisse werden anschließend an die Tafel geschrieben.

- **Winston Smith:** middle-aged, small, frail, thin body, rough and reddish complexion, fair hair, wearing a blue uniform, varicose ulcer
- **the inside of the apartment block:** cold, dusty, smelly, enormous posters of a middle-aged man on every landing, lift out of order
- **the outside of the apartment block:** posters of a middle-aged man with a moustache, reasonably handsome, a caption which reads "BIG BROTHER IS WATCHING YOU" (p. 39, l. 6), posters "plastered everywhere" (p. 39, ll. 3 f.), "from every commanding corner" (p. 39, ll. 4 f.), there is one poster just in front of Winston's window; very plain ("there seemed to be no color in anything", p. 39, ll. 2 f.); flat on the seventh floor, large windows; helicopters "snooping into people's windows" (p. 39, ll. 13 f.)
- **telesreen:** oblong metal plaque, producing noises, cannot be switched off completely ("[it] could be dimmed but there was no way of shutting it off completely", p. 38, ll. 30 f.), reading out figures

Wir schlagen nach der Auswertung der ersten Leseeindrücke einen Rückbezug zum Unterrichtseinstieg vor. Möglicher Impuls:

To what extent are Winston's freedoms restricted?

- there is no privacy, Winston feels being controlled (watched) in his flat
- he fears that his thoughts are controlled
- feels intimidated by the telescreen

Der Schluss des Texts sollte von den Schülerinnen und Schülern selbstständig auf der Grundlage der folgenden Verständnisfragen weitergelesen werden. Darüber hinaus sollte die oben begonnene Liste fortgesetzt werden.
Zusätzlich sollte jede Schülerin und jeder Schüler einen Satz oder kurzen Abschnitt auswählen, der über das gesellschaftliche Klima Ozeaniens eindrucksvoll Auskunft gibt.
Nun sind die Kursteilnehmerinnen und -teilnehmer im nächsten Unterrichtsabschnitt in der Lage, Ozeanien nochmals mit eigenen Worten zu beschreiben. Dabei stehen Aussagen zu folgenden Fragen im Vordergrund:

1. Who rules the people of Oceania?
2. What means are employed to maintain power over the people of Oceania?

1.
   - the totalitarian Big Brother government of Oceania and its large institutions (ministries), government officials are recruited from the state party
2.
   - the regime uses propaganda (slogans); its institutions, each concerned with a different aspect of people's everyday life, spread fear among the citizens
   - the government tries to control its citizens' everyday lift (*"Big Brother is watching you"* is just one example of many party slogans that implies the level of control we find in Oceania)

- the government uses various ways to catch people guilty of bad thoughts: the telescreen broadcasting party news as well as monitoring people in their homes (it cannot pick up noises such as whispering or scribbling though), helicopters and a vast army of informers called *Thought Police*, who watch every citizen at all times for the least signs of activities not in line with the government's agenda (unorthodox thoughts)
- huge Big Brother posters increase the feeling of intimidation in the people

Insbesondere der *telescreen* in Winstons Wohnung (wie in allen Wohnungen) steht für die perfiden Kontrollstrukturen des *Ministry of Truth.* Zur Vertiefung dieses Aspekts haben wir folgende kommunikative Übung eingesetzt:

How to sell a telescreen

Die Schülerinnen und Schüler sollen für einen neu entwickelten *telescreen* werben, der den Bedürfnissen des *Ministry of Truth,* dessen Funktion und Ziel nach der Lektüre bekannt ist, gerecht wird. Für die spätere Evaluation der Aktivität sollten vor der Erarbeitung der Produktwerbung Kriterien für einen akzeptablen *telescreen* im Sinne des *Ministry of Truth* aufgestellt und an der Tafel gesammelt werden.

Design (e.g. it's made of trendy disposable material and has a sophisticated design)

Size (e.g. it fits in every apartment but is large enough to capture everything going on inside the flat; enlarged field of vision)

Multi-functionality (e.g. it cannot be turned down below a certain minimum, so the thought-police can plug in unnoticed, and more people can be scrutinized at a certain time)

Reliability (e.g. it has a 5-year-guarantee, but can be fixed easily; there's a service number)

Efficiency (e.g. it detects every detail of people's activities inside the flat, can also pick up whispering and other noises that were not audible before (e.g. scribbling something on a sheet of paper))

Es hat sich folgender Ablauf als günstig erwiesen: Die Schülerinnen und Schüler entwerfen zunächst in Stammgruppen Merkmale eines neuen *telescreen,* der den o.g. Kriterien weitestgehend gerecht wird, visualisieren dann ihre Ideen *(outline plan)* und vereinbaren eine wirkungsvolle Verkaufsstrategie. Dabei soll jedes Gruppenmitglied in die Lage versetzt werden, die wichtigsten Merkmale des neuen Gerätes zu vermitteln. Die Produktpräsentation erfolgt in Expertengruppen mithilfe der *picture gallery-Methode,* d.h. die Gruppen werden neu zusammengesetzt – jedes Gruppenmitglied gehört nun einer anderen Expertengruppe an. Für die Präsentation werden die Poster *(outline plan)* im Klassenraum – wie in einer Galerie – verteilt; die Expertengruppen laufen von Plan zu Plan, der jeweilige Vertreter der Entwurfsgruppe präsentiert das Produkt. Auf diese Art und Weise sind die Schülerinnen und Schüler einmal Vortragende und ansonsten in der Rolle eines Vertreters des *Ministry of Truth* Zuhörer. Nach der Präsentation kehren die Schülerinnen und Schüler in ihre Stammgruppen zurück und wählen auf der Grundlage der vorher erarbeiteten Kriterien die überzeugendste Produktpräsentation aus. Ihre eigene Präsentation dürfen sie dabei nicht wählen. Folgender Impuls könnte von Ihnen vorgegeben werden:

How to sell a telescreen: You are a salesman for one of the leading telescreen producers in Oceania. Your company has just produced a new model of the telescreen, which is of much better quality and far more effective due to its features. Think of additional features which would make the most important control system of Oceania even more rigid. Develop a market strategy which will please the officials at the Ministry of Truth and make them declare your latest version of the telescreen compulsory for every household in Oceania. You are all travelling salespeople. Therefore, each group member must be able to present and promote your product. You should also draw an outline plan of your telescreen or a list of cues so that you can easily present your product and the representatives of the Ministry of Truth can follow your presentation more easily.

Charakteristisch für die Sprache Ozeaniens – vor allem auch im gewählten Textauszug – ist das von Orwell entwickelte *Newspeak* – die Manipulation der Sprache durch die Reduktion des Wortschatzes –, das zum Ziel hat, die Sprache frei zu machen von Mehrdeutigkeiten und Stilfiguren wie Ironie und Satire. Die sprachlichen Äußerungen der Bewohner Ozeaniens lassen sich so von der Partei besser kontrollieren. Für uns ausschlaggebend ist, dass die Sprache Ozeaniens theoretisch weiterentwickelt wurde und *Newspeak* heute quasi als Synonym für politisch gewollte Sprachmodifikationen (z. B. Wortverdrehungen, Euphemismen, Abkürzungen, Antithesen) steht. Langfristig geht mit diesen eine Veränderung im Denken der Sprecher einher, denn Phänomene, die sprachlich nicht ausgedrückt werden können, sind auch nicht denkbar – eine Theorie, die von den meisten Linguisten heute anerkannt wird. In Orwells Roman wird die Weltsicht der Bürger Ozeaniens stark von Wortschatz und Grammatik bestimmt.

Um die Bedeutung von *Newspeak* im gewählten Textauszug – und für das totalitäre Ozeanien – und damit einhergehend Orwells Wirkungsabsicht nachvollziehen zu können, schlagen wir die Bearbeitung eines zusätzlichen Sachtexts (s. *Copy 8*) zu semantischen und syntaktischen Strukturen von *Newspeak* und dessen Wirkung vor.

Der Text sollte zu Hause gelesen und die beiden *while-reading questions* schriftlich beantwortet werden. Leistungskursschülerinnen und -schüler könnten darüber hinaus bereits die unter dem Text stehende anspruchsvolle Aufgabe (*"Make a list of the linguistic features of Newspeak"*) bearbeiten. Im Grundkurs kann das alternativ zu Beginn der folgenden Stunde, ggf. in Gruppen, geschehen.

Lösungen zu *Copy 8*:

1. Newspeak was designed as the language with which the party (INGSOC – the English socialists) could best control the minds of the people of Oceania. This was achieved through changes to the semantic and syntactic structure of Standard English (Oldspeak), which was expected to have completely disappeared by the year 2050.
   The main idea was to diminish the number of words used. This was achieved through the reduction of words and the gradual elimination of irregularities (e.g. irregular verbs, antonyms, irregular plurals, etc.).

2. Some examples of Newspeak in the excerpt:

   hate week: probably a propaganda week directed against Oceania's enemies (p. 38, l. 15)

Excerpt from *The Principles of Newspeak* by George Orwell. An appendix to the novel *1984*

The appendix is written in the past as if Newspeak had been the world language for a number of years and Oldspeak had long been forgotten. Orwell's appendix sounds like an academic essay.

Newspeak was the official language of Oceania, and had been devised to meet the ideological needs of INGSOC, or English Socialism. In the year 1984 there was not as yet anyone who used Newspeak as his sole means of communication, either in speech or writing. The leading articles of the Times were written in it, but this was a tour de force which could only be carried out by a specialist. It was expected that Newspeak would have finally superseded Oldspeak (or standard English, as we should call it) by about the year 2050. Meanwhile, it gained ground steadily, all party members tending to use Newspeak words and grammatical constructions more and more in their everyday speech. The version in 1984, and embodied in the Ninth and Tenth Editions of the Newspeak dictionary, was a provisional one, and contained many superfluous words and archaic formations which were due to be suppressed later. It is with the final, perfected version, as embodied in the Eleventh Edition of the dictionary, that we are concerned here. The purpose of Newspeak was not only to provide a medium of expression for the world-view and mental habits proper to the devotees of INGSOC, but to make all other modes of thought impossible. It was intended that when Newspeak had been adopted once and for all and Oldspeak forgotten, a heretical thought – that is, a thought diverging from the principles of INGSOC – should be literally unthinkable, at least so far as thought is dependent on words. Its vocabulary was so constructed as to give exact and often very subtle expression to every meaning that a Party member could properly wish to express, while excluding all other meaning and also the possibility of arriving at them by indirect methods. This was done partly by the invention of new words, but chiefly by eliminating undesirable words and stripping such words as remained of unorthodox meanings, and so far as possible of all secondary meaning whatever. To give a single example, the word "free" still existed in Newspeak, but could only be used in such statements as "The dog is free from lice" or "This field is free from weeds." It could not be used in its old sense of "politically free" or "intellectually free," since political and intellectual freedom no longer existed even as concepts, and were therefore of necessity nameless. Quite apart from the suppression of definitely heretical words, reduction of vocabulary was regarded as an end in itself, and no word that could be dispensed with was allowed to survive.

Newspeak was designed not to extend but to diminish the range of thought, and this purpose was indirectly assisted by cutting the choice of words down to a minimum. Newspeak was founded on the English language as we know it, though many Newspeak sentences, even when not containing newly created words, would be barely intelligible to an English-speaker of our own day. [...]

The grammar of Newspeak has two outstanding peculiarities. The first of these was an almost complete interchangeability between different parts of speech. Any word in the language (in principle this applied even to very abstract words such as if or when) could be used either as verb, noun, adjective, or adverb. Between the verb and noun form, when of the same root, there was never any variation, this rule of itself involving the destruction of many archaic forms. The word thought, for example, did not exist in Newspeak. Its place was taken by think, which did duty for both noun and verb. [...]

Adjectives were formed by adding the suffix -ful to the noun verb, and adverbs by adding -wise. Thus, for example, speedful meant "rapid" and speedwise meant "quickly." Certain of our present-day adjectives, such as good, strong, big, black, soft, were retained, but their total number was very small. There was little need for them, since almost any adjectival meaning could be arrived at by adding -ful to a noun-verb. None of the now-existing adverbs was retained, except for a few already ending in -wise; the

to devise to plan, design

sole only

to supersede to replace

archaic formation expression, language structure characteristic of a more primitive period, here: standard English

to diverge to differ

What does Orwell say about the language spoken in Oceania in the year 1984 and what is his prediction for the future?

to eliminate to get rid of sth that is unnecessary or unwanted

What is the function of Newspeak?

heretical here: describing words and expressions which are not in line with the party's beliefs and convictions

to dispense with to manage without, here: redundant words

to diminish to reduce

-wise termination was invariable. The word well, for example, was replaced by goodwise. In addition, any word – this again applied in principle to every word in the language – could be negative by adding the affix un-, or could be strengthened by the affix plus-, or, for still greater emphasis doubleplus-. Thus, for example, uncold meant "warm" while pluscold and doublepluscold meant, respectively, "very cold" and "superlatively cold". It was also possible, as in present-day English, to modify the meaning of almost any word by prepositional affixes such as ante-, post-, up-, down-, etc. By such methods it was possible to bring about an enormous diminution of vocabulary. Given, for instance, the word good, there was no need for such a word as bad, since the required meaning was equally well – indeed better – expressed by ungood. All that was necessary, in any case where two words formed a natural pair of opposites, was to decide which of them to suppress. Dark, for example, could be replaced by unlight, or light by undark, according to preference.

diminution reduction

The second distinguishing mark of Newspeak grammar was its regularity. Subject to a few exceptions which are mentioned below, all inflections followed the same rules. Thus in all verbs the preterite and the past participle were the same and ended in -ed. The preterite of steal was stealed, the preterite of think was thinked, and so on throughout the language, all such forms as swam, gave, brought, spoke, taken, etc., being abolished. All plurals were made by adding -s or -es as the case might be. The plurals of man, ox, life, were mans, oxes, lifes. Comparison of adjectives was invariably made by adding -er, -est (good, gooder, goodest), irregular forms and the more, most formation being suppressed. [...]

preterite simple past

1. Make a list of the linguistic features of Newspeak (ll. 41 ff.) and compare them to what is called Oldspeak (Standard English). Pay special attention to semantic structures and syntactic structures. You can also go to www.en.wikipedia.org/wiki/Newspeak and www.newspeakdictionary.com to find out more about the idea and structure of Newspeak.
2. Start a list of examples of Newspeak you find in the given excerpt from *1984* and try to explain what they would be in Oldspeak.

INGSOC:	the English Socialists, the ruling party (p. 39, l. 10)
Miniluv:	Ministry of Love, "which maintained law and order" (p. 40, ll. 27f.)
Minipax:	Ministry of Peace (p. 40, ll. 26f.)
Minitrue:	Oceania's propaganda machine (p. 40, ll. 7ff.)
Miniplenty:	department of trade and industry (p. 40, ll. 28f.)
telescreen:	high-tech instrument for the complete surveillance of Oceania's population (p. 38, ll. 30f.)

Nach Besprechung der Hausaufgaben sollten die Kursteilnehmerinnen und Kursteilnehmer in der Lage sein, das Potenzial einer rigiden Sprachpolitik in repressiven politischen Systemen am Beispiel von *Newspeak* zu erläutern und auch die Aktualität dieser Problematik zu erkennen. Zusammenfassend könnte etwa folgender Absatz zur Ergebnissicherung an die Tafel geschrieben werden:

Newspeak is the official language of the totalitarian state of Oceania created by George Orwell. In Oceania, the state possesses control over every aspect of its citizens' everyday lives and, in particular, what they do in their free time, their social contacts and most and foremost their thoughts. Newspeak is the language that helps the government to achieve their goal of total control over the citizens of Oceania.

Zusätzlich könnten die Schülerinnen und Schüler noch für aktuelle Veränderungen in der Sprache sensibilisiert werden.

1. Newspeak today

Since Orwell wrote his book, Newspeak has been developed further, and nowadays, the term is seen as describing any political rhetoric that attempts to convey unpleasant political messages and make them sound more positive than they actually are. This is done through **politically-correct euphemisms, abbreviations and acronyms, misleading words and completely new words.** Try to uncover what is actually meant by the following words and phrases. They have been taken from www.newspeakdictionary.com.

Übertragen oder kopieren Sie die nachfolgende Tabelle auf eine Folie, verdecken Sie zunächst die rechte Spalte und fordern Sie Ihre Schülerinnen und Schüler auf, die neuenglischen Begriffe zu definieren.

dysfunctional family	(broken family)
behaviorally challenged	(misbehaved)
physically disadvantaged	(handicapped)
economically disadvantaged area	(slum)
freedom fighter	(soldier fighting against terrorists)
undocumented immigrants	(illegal immigrants)
visually challenging	(ugly)
losers of European descent	(white trash)

collateral damage	(civilians killed accidentally in military operations)
population transfer	(involuntary migration)
domestic engineer	(housewife)
administrative assistant	(secretary)

Zur Ergebnissicherung kann anschließend noch einmal die folgende Frage gestellt werden:

What is the difference between using the more recent terms on the left or the more traditional vocabulary on the right? Why – and by whom – might they have been invented and introduced into the English language?

In all cases, the more recent terms are euphemistic, palliative, or belittling. Governments or other authorities wanted human tragedies to sound more harmless (best examples: collateral damage, population transfer).

2. Zur Nachbereitung der Textarbeit lassen sich folgende Anknüpfungspunkte verfolgen: Die Schülerinnen und Schüler haben bereits herausgearbeitet, dass Winston die Legitimität der Parteilinie anzweifelt. Für diese Interpretation lassen sich zwar nur wenige Passagen im Textauszug finden, zur Einstimmung auf diese Übung sollten die Schülerinnen und Schüler jedoch auf die wenigen Beispiele verwiesen werden.

What is Winston's attitude towards the party line? Give evidence from the text when you explain.

p. 39, ll. 32f.: "Winston kept his back turned to the telescreen. It was safer, though, as he well knew, even a back can be revealing."
p. 39, ll. 38ff.: "He tried to squeeze out some childhood memory…" (We would assume that the Party doesn't want Winston to question his level of satisfaction with his current reality.

Im weiteren Verlauf des Romans würden die Schülerinnen und Schüler auf Emmanuel Goldstein stoßen, der sich von einem hochrangigen Parteimitglied zu einem Dissidenten und Gegner der Partei entwickelt hat. Goldstein ist inzwischen ein führender Vertreter des innerstaatlichen Widerstands. Zusätzlich könnten Sie – oder ein Referent aus dem Kreis der Kursteilnehmerinnen und Kursteilnehmer – den weiteren Romanverlauf zusammenfassen: Winston beginnt ein Tagebuch und eine Liebesbeziehung – beide Vorgänge bedeuten eine Abkehr von der Parteilinie –, um schließlich zu folgendem kreativen Schreibimpuls überzuleiten:

A letter to Emmanuel Goldstein

Although this is virtually impossible, Winston hears of Emmanuel Goldstein, once a high-ranking party official, who now is a leading force in the resistance movement. Winston has grown suspicious of the legitimacy of the order in Oceania and is not convinced of the validity of instruments used by the Ministry of Truth. Compose Winston's letter to Goldstein in which he states his doubts and raises questions as to the purpose and legitimacy of the Ministry of Truth and asks for details about Goldstein's resignation from his party post.

3. Darüber hinaus könnten Sie das Phänomen der *Big Brother shows* thematisieren und mithilfe eines *prompt* eine lebhafte Diskussion anstoßen. Dazu eignet sich wiederum ein *prompt*, der in kurzer Stillarbeit beendet werden soll. Dieser könnte lauten:

If I were offered a huge sum of money to join the Big Brother Camp, I would ...

Zu erwarten ist, dass viele, wenn nicht sogar alle Schülerinnen und Schüler Ihrer Lerngruppe eine Teilnahme an einem *Big Brother*-Programm ablehnen. Daher lässt sich die Diskussion fortführen, indem Sie einen weiteren *prompt* vorgeben und anschließend über die Motive einer Teilnahme diskutieren:

However, I might agree to join the program if I ...

Als Hausaufgabe zur nächsten Stunde sollten der erste Text von Margaret Atwood, also der Auszug aus *The Handmaid's Tale* gelesen und die *while-reading questions* beantwortet werden.

Component 4

The present

4.1 After the catastrophe: Margaret Atwood, *The Handmaid's Tale*

Hinweis: Zu diesem Roman liegt in der EinFach-Englisch-Reihe des Schöningh Verlages ein eigenes Unterrichtsmodell vor (ISBN 978-3-14-041208-7).

Margaret Atwoods *The Handmaid's Tale* ist in vielerlei Sicht vergleichbar mit den Textauszügen im dritten Kapitel der Textausgabe, wenn die Autorin auch andere Akzente setzt und die Protagonisten jeweils unterschiedlich mit den totalitären Strukturen und Repressionen in ihren Gesellschaften umgehen. Alle drei Autoren in Kapitel III. befassen sich aber mit den düsteren Zukunftsszenarien, die dem Zusammenbruch ziviler Strukturen auf dem technologischen Höhepunkt der Gesellschaft folgen. Man könnte sagen, Atwoods Handlung setzt zeitlich dort an, wo die anderen Autoren aufhören. Technische Innovationen, die bei Huxley und Orwell noch pure Spekulationen waren, sind für Margaret Atwood zur konkreten Alltagserfahrung geworden und haben bereits Gegenströmungen hervorgerufen, die sich im politischen Diskurs der nordamerikanischen Gesellschaft wiederfinden.
Ort der Romanhandlung ist die Republik Gilead, deren Regierungsgeschäfte von einer Gruppe von Fundamentalisten, auf deren Identität die Autorin nicht konkret eingeht, übernommen wird. Die neuen Technologien werden vor allem eingesetzt, um Frauen zu entrechten und zu entmündigen, die Erfolge der Frauenbewegung umzukehren und eine autoritäre, patriarchalische Gesellschaftsordnung zu verwirklichen.
Zum besseren Textverständnis des gewählten Ausschnitts sollten die Kursteilnehmerinnen und -teilnehmer darauf hingewiesen werden, dass das Schaffen der kanadischen Autorin von der Frauenbewegung der 1970er-Jahre, ihren Gegenbewegungen und natürlich auch ihren Erfahrungen auf Reisen nach Afghanistan, in den Iran und nach Osteuropa geprägt ist. Atwoods Beobachtungen zu Amerikas *New Right Movement,* die auch in der Gegenwart politische Foren nutzt, um Einfluss auf gesellschaftsrelevante Entscheidungen zu nehmen, sowie ihre Auseinandersetzung mit jeder Art von religiösem Fundamentalismus fließen ebenfalls in ihre Texte ein.
So lassen sich auch in der Gegenwart intellektuelle Gegenbewegungen ausmachen. Fernsehprediger und Bibelexperten genießen inzwischen nicht nur in den USA ein hohes Ansehen; sie stellen ihre Vorstellungen zum Verhältnis der Geschlechter auf die Grundlage des Evangeliums und argumentieren, dass Frauen erst durch die Frauenbewegung, die das traditionelle Rollenverhältnis diffamiert habe, in die unbefriedigende Lage gekommen seien, einer oft schlecht bezahlten Erwerbstätigkeit nachgehen und gleichzeitig für die Familie sorgen zu müssen, statt sich auf ihre Aufgaben im Haushalt konzentrieren zu können.

Im ausgewählten Auszug erinnert sich Offred, die Protagonistin des Romans, an die Etablierung des fundamentalistischen Regimes Gileads, also an die Zeit, als Frauen ersten Repressalien unterworfen werden. In einem *flashback,* einem literarischen Mittel, das Atwood den Roman hindurch einsetzt, durchlebt sie die kleinen Schritte ihrer Entmündigung nochmals und die Leserinnen und Leser erfahren auch, wie unterschiedlich die Bewohner Gileads damit umgehen: Während Offreds Partner Luke beschwichtigt und die Veränderungen als notwendig

für die Aufrechterhaltung von Sicherheit und Ordnung akzeptiert, analysiert Moira, eine radikale Feministin, die Maßnahmen als Anschlag auf die Unabhängigkeit der Frau.
Die Schülerinnen und Schüler sollten den Text mithilfe der *while-reading questions* zu Hause vorbereitend erarbeitet haben. Zur Überprüfung der Hausaufgabe können Sie folgende fehlerhafte Zusammenfassung auf eine Folie oder auf *Handouts* kopieren und in Partner- oder Einzelarbeit berichtigen lassen.

Flawed summary:

In this chapter, Offred recalls the political takeover in Gilead, which brought a new government to power which amends the constitution and takes other steps to improve the position of women. Islamic fundamentalists are responsible for the coup, but according to newspaper reports, the suspects of the coup are tracked down by special police units and the upheaval is put to an end.
Offred is working at a library where she issues historical and political volumes and assists people with finding information in them. One morning, on her way to work, Offred stops at the store to buy a pack of cigarettes. There she is served by a young man who tells her that the female clerk who has worked there up till then has unexpectedly been sent into early retirement. She is surprised to learn that her bank account doesn't have sufficient funding so that she is unable to obtain any cash. The same day, Offred's employer tells her that she has to transfer to another department in the library.
Luke, a close friend of Offred's, is startled at the news and advises her to contact the unions. Although Offred is worried, she seems to accept the status quo. Later that day, Offred talks to her mother who tells her that all steps for monitoring people's cash-flow have been taken by government officials to track down every individual no matter where they are. She willingly adjusts to her new status.

Lösungsvorschlag für ein korrigiertes *summary*:

The President and Congress are executed and certain supposedly "temporary" restrictions are put into place such as the suspension of the constitution, the closure or censorship of newspapers and the installation of roadblocks to maintain peace and stability in the Republic of Gilead. Islamic terrorists are blamed for the coup but officials never provide any evidence regarding the truth of the accusations.
Offred is working at a library but her job is to transfer books to computer discs so that they can later be eliminated. On her way to work one day, she stops by at the corner-shop where she is usually served by a grey-haired woman who is about her mother's age. But that day there is a young man, who not only doesn't know anything about the woman's disappearance, he also tells Offred that her money card is invalid. When she arrives at work her boss, who is visibly shocked at the new regulations, tells all female employees that they can no longer work there. Offred is later told that women are not allowed to have any possessions and that their money has been transferred to their husband's accounts. Being unable to get in touch with her mother, Offred manages to talk to her friend Moira, who explains the government's intention of denying women civil rights in the aftermath of the coup: they want to prevent them from leaving the country. Luke is not supportive. In fact, he is also

indifferent to the long-term consequences of the political takeover, and easily slides into the role of the sole-breadwinner of the family. Offred also remains ignorant although she quietly struggles with her new role as a housewife. We also learn that Offred's mother has taken a more active role in the political struggle against the regime.

Der Text bietet eine Reihe gegenwartsrelevanter Anknüpfungspunkte, weshalb wir zur thematischen Vertiefung des Auszugs, der sprachlich problemlos auch von Grundkursen zu bewältigen ist, Zusatztexte eingesetzt haben.
Besonders kontrovers sind in diesem Zusammenhang die Thesen von Phyllis Schlafly und Jerry Falwell. Schlafly ist eine der prominentesten Publizistinnen des amerikanischen *New Right Movement*, das seit über 30 Jahren mit seinen Stellungnahmen zu aktuellen Themen der Innenpolitik vor allem die Ziele der Frauenbewegung attackiert beziehungsweise diffamiert. Auch Falwell, ein über die Grenzen Virginias hinaus bekannter Prediger, kritisierte seinerzeit die geplante Verfassungsänderung zur gesellschaftlichen Gleichstellung der Geschlechter, weil sie gegen die göttliche Vorbestimmung der Rolle von Mann und Frau im Zusammenleben und gegen die Institution der Familie gerichtet sei, und unterstützt auch gegenwärtig, genau wie Schlafly, publikumswirksam die Kampagnen des *New Right Movement.* Nach den Anschlägen auf das World Trade Center in New York sah er sogar die Frauen- und Bürgerrechtsbewegung in der Verantwortung für die Katastrophe, als er ausführte:
"I really believe that the pagans, and the abortionists, and the feminists, and the gays and the lesbians who are actively trying to make that an alternative lifestyle, the ACLU [American Civil Liberties Union], People For the American Way, all of them who have tried to secularize America. I point the finger in their face and say 'you helped this happen'."[1]
Um den Schülerinnen und Schülern einen Einblick in die Breite der Argumentation Falwells und anderer (Fernseh-)Prediger zu verschaffen, lohnt es sich, weitere Falwell-Zitate zu präsentieren und auf die zunehmende Popularität des christlichen Fundamentalismus in den USA hinzuweisen. Lassen Sie die Zusatztexte auf *Copy 9* arbeitsteilig im Unterricht lesen und unter folgenden Fragestellungen bearbeiten:

1. Summarize the author's main arguments.
2. What stylistic means does the author use to convince his/her readers?

[1] http://en.wikiquote.org/wiki/Jerry_Falwell

The fundamentalist "New Right Movement"

I. From Phyllis Schlafly's Report, december 2004 (vol. 38, no. 5)

Stay-at-Home Moms Back in Style

When Time Magazine runs a cover story called "The Case for Staying Home," and Reuters reports that housework is good for women because it can help prevent ovarian cancer, you know the feminists are on the run. Stay-at-home moms are coming back in style.

Time reports that there has been a dramatic "drop-off" in workplace participation by married mothers with infants less than a year old. The figure fell from 59 % in 1997 to 53 % in 2000, and the drop was mostly among well-educated women over age 30. It's big news that more mothers are dropping off the corporate or professional ladder, and that fewer babies are dropped off at daycare.

According to an Australian-Chinese study published in the International Journal of Cancer, moderate exercise such as housework decreases the risk of ovarian cancer in women. The more and the harder the housework the housewife does, the more she benefits. [...]

Why you won't read optimistic news like this in the major women's magazines is entertainingly explained in the book by Myrna Blyth, editor-in-chief of *Ladies' Home Journal* for two decades, called *Spin Sisters: How the Women of the Media Sell Unhappiness and Liberalism to the Women of America.*

The Spin Sisters are the high-profile women in the media, both those who control the profitable women's magazines and the anorexic female hosts on television. They are all busy selling American women the ideology of victimhood, the attitude that women's lives are full of misery and threats, and that women suffer from a constant state of stress that keeps them unable to cope with life's ordinary irritations.

The whole premise of female victimhood is false. American women today live longer, healthier lives than ever, filled with a multitude of opportunities for education, travel and employment. The feminist movement flowered in the 1970s, powered by Betty Friedan's invitation for fulltime homemakers to be liberated from an oppressive patriarchal society and the home she described as a "comfortable concentration camp." The purveyors of such radical rhetoric have grown old and tiresome, but their thesis has been eagerly espoused by the Spin Sisters, who have learned how to market victimhood for rich profits and their own luxurious lifestyle. [...]

Today's Spin Sisters tell women that they are living in a treacherous stress-filled world, confronted by threats from everything from abusive husbands to contaminated foods in their refrigerator. Women's worry list of fears and woes includes everything from the weight of the world's problems to the weight of extra fat on themselves. A typical article in a woman's magazine is "The Health Hazard in Your Handbag."

Ms. Blyth describes how the Spin Sisters on the TV networks (Barbara, Katie, Diane, Connie, etc.) are not really rivals, but are a Girls' Club with a mission. Abortion is their bonding factor; the Spin Sisters will never allow any challenge to it to emerge on their television screens or their magazine pages. The Girls' Club orchestrated a media campaign to promote their favorites Rosie O'Donnell, Hillary Clinton, and Jane Fonda. [...]

Bernard Goldberg lifted the curtain on the how the media peddle the feminist promotion of daycare in his best-selling book *Bias*. He wrote that "the most important story you never saw on TV" is "the terrible things that are happening to America's children" because "mothers have opted for work outside of the house over taking care of their children at home." [...]

http://www.eagleforum.org

drop-off/drop reduction

to drop off the corporate ladder to suddenly leave a professional career

to drop off at daycare to leave a child at a kindergarten

premise idea, belief on which sth is based

purveyor here: advocate, provider

to espouse to follow (ideas)

contaminated poisoned

Rosie O'Donnell American actress, talk-show host and comedian. She is an outspoken critic of contemporary issues such as the Iraq war and gun-control in America.

Hillary Clinton Democratic United States Senator, wife of former US President Bill Clinton

Jane Fonda American actress, writer and political activist, who campaigned against the Vietnam War and has been involved in the Feminist Movement since the 1970s

to peddle here: to try to persuade audiences or talk them into sth

II. Jerry Falwell sees feminism as a threat to the American family, 1980

From *Listen, America* by Jerry Falwell

[...] There is a vicious assault upon the American family. More television programs depict homes of divorced or of single parents than depict the traditional family. Nearly every major family-theme TV program openly justifies divorce, homosexuality, and adultery. Some sociologists believe that the family unit, as we know it, could disappear by the year 2000. [...]

In the war against the family today, we find an arsenal of weapons. The first weapon is the cult of the playboy, the attitude that has permeated our society in these last twenty years. This playboy philosophy tells men that they do not have to be committed to their wife and to their children, but that they should be some kind of a "cool, free swinger." Sexual promiscuity has become the life style of America. The cult of the playboy is more than just a revolution of dirty magazines. It represents a life style that ultimately corrupts the family. Men are satisfying their lustful desires at the expense of family.

The second weapon against the family is the feminist revolution. This is the counter-reaction to the cult of the playboy. Many women are saying, "Why should I be taken advantage of by chauvinists? I will get out and do my own thing. I will stand up for my rights. I will have my own dirty magazines." Feminists are saying that self-satisfaction is more important than the family. Most of the women who are leaders in the feminist movement promote an immoral life style.

In a drastic departure from the home, more than half of the women in our country are currently employed. Our nation is in serious danger when motherhood is considered a task that is "unrewarding, unfulfilling, and boring." I believe that a woman's call to be a wife and mother is the highest calling in the world. My wife is proud to be called a housewife. She is dedicated to making a happy and rich life for us and our three children. She does not consider her life work of making my life happy and that of loving and shaping the lives of our precious children inconsequential or demeaning. Women who choose to remain in the home should never feel inferior to those working outside, but should know they are fulfilling God's command for the home [...].

Many women today say that they must work for economic reasons. Although inflation has placed a financial burden on the family, we are overly concerned about materialistic wealth. Many Americans consider it more important to have several cars in the driveway, a beautiful house, and two color television sets than to have a stable home environment for their children.

[...] The answer to stable families with children who grow up to be great leaders in our society and who themselves have stable homes will not come from, as Judy Mann states, more part-time work for fathers and mothers, or parental leaves of absence, or thirty-hour weeks, or parental cooperatives and other forms of sharing child-raising responsibilities. It will come only as men and women in America get in a right relationship to God and His principles for the home ....

The Scripture declares that God has called the father to be the spiritual leader in his family. The husband is not to be the dictator of the family, but the spiritual leader. There is a great difference between a dictator and a leader. People follow dictators because they are forced to do so. They follow leaders because they want to. Good husbands who are godly men are good leaders. Their wives and children want to follow them and be under their protection. The husband is to be the decision-maker and the one who motivates his family with love. The Bible says that husbands are to love their wives even as Christ also loved the church and gave Himself for it. [...]

Until men are in right relationship with God, there is no hope for righting our families of our nation. Because we have weak men we have weak homes, and children from these homes will probably grow up to become weak parents leading even weaker homes.

http://american.edu/bgriff/H207web/fem/AdditionalDocsonFeminismMP1992.htm#falwell

assault attack

to depict to show

to permeate to spread

promiscuity the habit of having frequently changing partners

demeaning here: degrading

to right to correct, return to a proper position

Die Antworten sollten von den Schülerinnen und Schülern auf Folien oder an die Tafel geschrieben werden.

	Phyllis Schlafly	Jerry Falwell
Main arguments:	• there is an increasing number of women who choose to stay out of jobs and disagree with the concepts of the feminist movement • positive stories about women who decide to opt out of jobs and become housewives are barred from news coverage • there is a conspiracy that includes successful business women and politicians of the political left advocating the idea of feminism and condemning traditional role models only to seek their own advantages • feminists are successfully advocating the idea that women live in misery and victimhood • it's mainly the children who suffer when their mothers go out to work	• the institution of the American family is threatened by various factors such as the macho-culture and the feminist revolution • campaigners in the feminist movement promote immorality and advocate women working outside their homes, thereby neglecting their families • many Americans seek material well-being rather than harmony in their homes • the Christian faith demands that men and women adopt traditional roles, the husband being the leader of the family • the family as the backbone of society can only be rescued if people revive their faith
Stylistic means:	• makes references to publicly-known women (e.g. TV personalities and politicians without giving their full name) • refers to other writers (recently-published texts) • provides data and sources • uses arguments only to prove the opposite	• author employs figurative and metaphoric language ("the family is threatened by an arsenal of weapons") • the text is packed with religious symbols and images • makes references to other authors • makes predictions • employs simple and repetitive language

Nach der inhaltlichen Textsicherung haben wir weitere Methoden eingesetzt, mithilfe derer sich die Schüler produktiv (aus unterschiedlichen Perspektiven) mit den Thesen Schlaflys und Falwells auseinandersetzen können. Auf der Grundlage der hier ausgewählten Zitate könnten Sie eine *public debate* (vgl. *Copy 4)* initiieren, in der die Kursteilnehmer und -teilnehmerinnen entweder die Position Schlaflys oder die einer Vertreterin der Frauenbewegung (bezogen auf den Textauszug z. B. von Offreds Freundin Moira oder Offreds Mutter) einnehmen:

Mögliche Themenstellungen:

- "Sex education classes are like in-home sales parties for abortions."
- "Sexual harassment on the job is not a problem for virtuous women."
- "What I am defending is the real rights of women. A woman should have the right to be in the home as a wife and mother."
- "Feminism is doomed to failure because it is based on an attempt to repeal and restructure human nature."[1]

Alternativ könnten die Zitate auch zum Ausgangspunkt einer schriftlichen Ausarbeitung werden: Geben Sie eines der Zitate entweder als ersten oder letzten Satz einer Rede Schlaflys vor; die Schüler verfassen die komplette Rede, indem sie wieder die Ziele und Erfolge der Frauen- und Bürgerrechtsbewegung kritisch hinterfragen bzw. denunzieren. Auf diesem Wege könnten sie auch ein Gespür für die Popularität des *New Right Movement* in Teilen der (amerikanischen) Gesellschaft bekommen und üben sich in der Verwendung von Stilmitteln.

Der Text könnte auch an die Protagonistin im Textauszug gerichtet sein, indem er die politischen Vorgänge, insbesondere die Entrechtung der Frauen, in Gilead rechtfertigt und die Homosexualität Moiras als unmoralisch und pervers verurteilt. So würde sich ein Rückbezug zum Textauszug ergeben.

Um die Schülerinnen und Schüler abschließend zu einer persönlichen Stellungnahme zur inhaltlichen Auseinandersetzung mit dem Textauszug zu bewegen, bieten sich folgende *prompts* an:

What-if:

- your country was invaded by a foreign power?
- your government was overthrown by an extremist group?
- civil liberties were restricted in order to restore order?
- women were forced to stay out of jobs?
- women were not allowed to have private possessions?

Auch wenn Atwoods Vorstellungen extrem sind, sollten die Schülerinnen und Schüler abschließend nochmals zum Gegenwartsbezug der Entwicklungen in Gilead Stellung nehmen. Dabei könnte die Diskussion auf eine aktuelle Kontroverse (vor allem in den USA) gelenkt werden: dem Widerspruch zwischen staatlichen Kontrollmechanismen zur Aufrechterhaltung von Sicherheit und Ordnung auf der einen Seite und dem Schutz individueller Freiheitsrechte nach den Anschlägen vom 11. September 2001 in Amerikas Kampf gegen den internationalen Terrorismus auf der anderen Seite.

---

[1] Diese und weitere Zitate finden Sie hier: http://thinkexist.co/quotes/phyllis_schlafly

4.2 It is the world that has been pulled over your eyes to blind you from the truth: Larry and Andy Wachowski, *The Matrix*

Mit Gesamteinnahmen von ca. 456 Millionen Dollar weltweit und vier *Academy Awards* für technische Innovationen gehört die *Matrix*-Trilogie zu den überzeugendsten Werken der Filmgeschichte. Im Mittelpunkt der Handlung steht Neo (in *The Matrix* Thomas Anderson), der einerseits als gewöhnlicher Programmierer in einem IT-Unternehmen tätig ist, andererseits unter dem Pseudonym „Neo" ein Leben als Hacker führt.
Eines Tages wird er von Morpheus gefunden, dem Führer einer Untergrundorganisation, der ihm offenbart, dass die Menschheit in einer von Computern gesteuerten Scheinwelt (der Matrix) leben würde. Neo sei bestimmt, sie aus den Fängen der Maschinen zu befreien. Der Film enthält religiöse, philosophische und politische Bezüge und ist wiederum Ausdruck des Technikpessimismus', der Kapitalismuskritik (hic. der Angst vor der Macht mächtiger Konzerne und der Endlichkeit der Energieressourcen) und der Ohnmacht gegenüber einem System der von den Medien geschaffenen Illusionswelt von Bildern, Filmen und Computerspielen. Damit trägt der Film deutlich dystopische Züge: Der Zuschauer wird mit einer Zukunftswelt konfrontiert, in der nicht der Mensch Herr der Maschinen ist, sondern in der nach der Zerstörung der wichtigsten Lebensgrundlagen die Maschinen unterstützt von menschlichen Assistenten *(Agents)* die Menschheit künstlich am Leben erhalten. Nur die kleine Gruppe um Morpheus versucht dieses System nachhaltig zu stören. Die für die Textausgabe ausgewählte Sequenz steht am Anfang des Films und sei hier knapp zusammengefasst:
Neo erwacht scheinbar aus einem Alptraum, in dem er in einem kahlen Raum von Agenten verhört und verwanzt wird. Kurz darauf nimmt Morpheus telefonisch Kontakt zu Neo auf, um ein Treffen zu arrangieren. Auf dem Weg dorthin entfernt Trinity zunächst die Wanze, woraus ersichtlich wird, dass es sich bei dem Verhör um einen realen Vorgang gehandelt haben muss.
Bei ihrer ersten Begegnung konfrontiert Morpheus Neo mit der Behauptung, die Welt sei ein Trugbild, eine Illusion (die Matrix), und stellt ihn vor die Wahl, entweder in die Normalität (die Scheinwelt) zurückzukehren oder aber den Versuch zu unternehmen, die Wahrheit über die Matrix und die dahinterstehenden Kräfte herauszufinden. Neo entscheidet sich für die Wahrheit. Er wird noch einmal geboren, findet sich in der Matrix wieder, erkennt die Macht der Maschinen, wird aber von Morpheus' Crew gerettet und an Bord der *Nebukadnezar* gebracht. Morpheus erzählt Neo die Geschichte der Matrix, die zu Beginn des 21. Jahrhunderts geschaffen worden sei, als die Menschen in ihrer Nachlässigkeit die Kontrolle über die Maschinen verloren hätten. Diese würden die Menschen nun in einer Traumwelt am Leben erhalten, um sie als Energiequellen zu nutzen. Noch zweifelt Neo an Morpheus' Ausführungen, womit die Sequenz endet. Nicht nur Neo stellt sich die Frage: *What is the Matrix?*

Die Schülerinnen und Schüler sollten zum besseren Seh- bzw. Hörverständnis den Ausschnitt aus dem Filmskript (Textausgabe S. 52–63) vor der Filmanalyse gelesen haben. Wir schlagen vor, dass das Leseverständnis mithilfe der *True/False statements* von *Copy 10* auf der inhaltlichen Ebene gesichert wird.

Lösungsvorschläge zu *Copy 10*:

1. Probably false because Trinity removes the bug that has been planted in his stomach during the interrogation.
2. False. They are more likely to be secret agents because of their attire and their behaviour.

3. True.
4. True.
5. False. He's accompanied by Trinity; Morpheus awaits him.
6. False. The meeting place is located in the ruined city of Chicago and is deserted; the meeting is obviously held in secret.
7. False. The action must be set sometime in the 22nd century. There is reference to this in the sequel: Morpheus says that he doesn't know the exact date but it must be about 2199.
8. False. Although Neo remains doubtful at first, he is also curious and determined to find out the truth about the nature of the Matrix.
9. True.
10. True.
11. True.
12. False. Morpheus and his crew travel on a hovercraft called "The Nebuchadnezzar".
13. True but the machines have human helpers, such as Agent Smith.

Während des ersten Sehens achten die Schülerinnen und Schüler auf Filmelemente (Objekte), die deutlich machen, dass die Handlung in der Zukunft (ca. 2199) spielt:

What elements of the scene indicate that *The Matrix* is set in the future?

Als Einhilfen könnten Kategorien *(physical features, human aspects, the function/role of machines)* vorgegeben werden. Natürlich könnte die Lektüre des Skriptauszugs auch jetzt erst erfolgen. Die Antworten sollten zur Ergebnissicherung an die Tafel geschrieben werden.

physical features: the city of Chicago ruined, eternal darkness, wasteland, dark sky

human aspects: humans in pods resembling each other, reproduced and supplied by machines, loss of diversity [the computer agents resemble each other, too], artificiality, disillusionment

machines: robots dominating (ruling) humans

Dem Einsatz der Farben kommt im gesamten Film eine besondere Bedeutung zu; durch sie lassen sich Spieler und Gegenspieler, die Welt innerhalb und außerhalb der Matrix und ihre Vertreter zuordnen und der Film (die Sequenz) verstehen. Wir sind sogar der Meinung, dass in *The Matrix* Farben das wichtigste filmische Mittel sind, daher wenden wir uns in diesem Unterrichtsmodell – anders als die meisten anderen Filmanalysen – vor allem diesem sonst vernachlässigten Aspekt zu. Weitere filmische Mittel sollten an dieser Szene nicht untersucht werden, da nach unserer Erfahrung Schülerinnen und Schüler die Freude an der Filmanalyse verlieren, wenn Szenen allzu oft gesehen werden. Die Filmanalyse soll nicht zum Selbstzweck werden, sondern diejenigen Mittel untersuchen, die zum Verständnis der jeweiligen Handlung beitragen und mithilfe derer sich der Zuschauer die Motive der technischen Entschei-

True/False statements

Are the following statements true or false?
Correct what you consider wrong.

1. Neo experiences a nightmare at the beginning of the sequence.

2. He is interrogated by police cops who ask him to cooperate with the police.

3. Neo leads a double life as Thomas Anderson and Neo, the hacker.

4. Agent Smith thinks that Neo can lead him to Morpheus and his underground rebel group.

5. Neo is picked up by Morpheus and taken to meet Trinity for the first time.

6. Neo is taken to a public building inside a technology park.

7. The action is set at the end of the 20th century.

8. Neo is a hesitant and insecure young man.

9. Neo is reborn and escapes the Matrix.

____

____

10. While he is being reproduced, Neo sees human batteries filled with red gelatine which are connected to each other.

____

____

11. Chicago as it was in the 20th century no longer exists, but the people in the Matrix cannot see the truth.

____

____

12. Morpheus and his crew travel on a submarine called "The Nebuchadnezzar".

____

____

13. At the end of the 20th century, mankind experienced a natural disaster and lost control over the machines which then set up an invincible network run without humans at all.

____

____

dungen des Regisseurs bewusst machen kann. Die verschiedenen Kamerapositionen (und im Falle von *The Matrix* besonders Mittel der Filmmontage wie *fade, dissolve, cross-cuts, jump cuts, match cuts*) können stattdessen in den ersten Szenen (Trinitys Verfolgung durch Matrix-Agenten) analysiert werden. An dieser Stelle könnte auch auf die häufigen Schnitte und deren Effekte eingegangen werden.
Rot, Grün (hierbei handelt es sich um ein eher mattes Grün bzw. Giftgrün), Schwarz und Weiß sind ständig wiederkehrende Farben im Film. Zum Einstieg in die Farbanalyse schlagen wir zunächst eine Wortschatzübung zur Verwendung von Farben in idiomatischen Wendungen vor. Die folgende Übung sollte an die Tafel geschrieben oder auf eine Folie kopiert werden.

Choose from the colours given.

1. She was ____________ with anger. (white/green/blue)
2. The news came out of the ____________. We were all shocked. (blue/ red/ white)
3. A ____________ letter day is a special one. (blue/red)
4. I'm overdrawn again. My bank account is in the ____________. (red/black)
5. I was ____________ with envy. (blue/green/black)
6. It seems impossible for me to get a bank loan. I must be on a ____________ list. (red/black/blue)
7. It looks like we will be taken over by our rivals unless a ____________ knight steps in with a higher bid. (black/white)
8. Everybody in the office said that my marriage would fail so there were a few ____________ faces when it worked out. (blue/green/red)
9. It's her first day in the office, so she is really ____________. (blue/green/white)
10. It was a ____________ day for me when I lost my friend. (red/white/black)
11. When your bank account is in credit, you are in the ____________. (red/black)

Lösungen:

1. white	4. red	7. white	10. black
2. blue	5. green	8. red	11. black
3. red	6. black	9. green	

Darüber hinaus haben die Schülerinnen und Schüler natürlich eigene, sich z. T. auch widersprechende Assoziationen zur Wirkung von Farben. Je nach Intensität (es werden z. B. mindestens dreißig Rottöne unterschieden) lassen sich Farben mit unterschiedlichen Bildern verknüpfen. Bevor wir konkret auf die Sequenz eingehen, verteilen wir im Klassenraum Buntpapier in (unterschiedlichen) Grüntönen, Rottönen, Schwarz und Weiß. Die Kursteilnehmer bewegen sich (still) im Raum und notieren (individuell) auf jeweils bereitliegenden Blättern alle Assoziationen und Vergleiche, die ihnen zu den Farben einfallen; auch Situationsbeispiele oder Redewendungen können notiert werden (z. B. *black reminds me of mourning and funerals; to be in the red).* Dabei werden sie bereits selbst auf ambivalente Assoziationen stoßen, d. h. einerseits lösen Farben positive *(red reminds me of roses, love and passion),* andererseits negative Gefühle aus *(red is also a symbol of aggression and war [blood]).* Besonders reizvoll ist diese Bestandsaufnahme natürlich, wenn die Lerngruppe multikulturell ist. Einzelne Schülerinnen/Schüler präsentieren dann die gesammelten Assoziationen.

Possible associations:

Green: hope, nature, purity, sexuality/fertility (spring), peace, rebirth, (economic recovery), but also evil, envy and poisonous substances (chemicals, drugs)

Red: love (heart), compassion, obsession, desire, start/beginning, power, birth, the passion of life, but also murder (blood), tension, chaos and danger (e.g. traffic lights, fire, poison)

Black: darkness, misery, decay, end, secrecy, evil, mourning and grieving (death)

White: truth, purity, sterility (hospital, church), emptiness, (political) neutrality, precision, (godlike) holiness, the good, eternity, beginning, artificiality, wealth

Beim nochmaligen Sehen der Sequenz achten die Schüler und Schülerinnen auf den Einsatz der Farbmittel und ihrer Bedeutung. Dabei sollten Sie der Lerngruppe die Eingangssequenz *(Trinity's phone trace)* nicht vorenthalten. In ihr wird bereits die Farbe Grün (Matrix-Code) hervorgehoben. Zunächst sollen Objekte aufgelistet werden. Im Unterrichtsgespräch diskutieren die Kursteilnehmer und -teilnehmerinnen dann den zielgerichteten Einsatz der Farbmittel, erkennen ihre Bedeutung in *The Matrix,* können schließlich die Handlungszusammenhänge verstehen und die Ausgangsfrage *(What is the Matrix?)* beantworten. Es empfiehlt sich, arbeitsteilig vorzugehen. Die Lerngruppe erkennt, dass der zielgerichtete Einsatz der Farben zur Strukturierung des Films beiträgt.

	objects	meaning
black	• the city on their way to Morpheus, Chicago in reality (in 2199) • sunglasses and coats of the agents and the crew	• the destruction of human life, hiding from being discovered by the agents (the crew) • hiding vulnerability / showing the power (over those who are not willing to comply to the rules of the Matrix (interrogation room, agents)) and being invincible
white	• the crew on the Nebuchadnezzar, outside the Matrix	• Everything outside the Matrix is clean, sterile and free; it is the refuge of only a few humans and human life; there they are safe.
red	• the red pill • blood (the pods the babies are kept in and the membrane surrounding them, Neo awakes in red liquid) • the armchairs (Morpheus tells Neo about the Matrix)	• The pill saves Neo and gives him a new life (a new identity); he is seen as the savior by the crew (he will be able to fight the Matrix); it gives humans new life (but only to be kept in a state of slavery or bondage).
(acid) green	• Matrix Code • Neo's computer screen • the interrogation room • the wax running down Neo's hand and creeping up his body • used throughout the entire sequence (film)	• The Matrix (is a simulated, computerized, artificial world); humans are produced and kept alive by computers; the green background suggests that the world as it seems to most humans is controlled by a network of computers which is invincible.

Im Anschluss an die Analyse schlagen wir eine kreative Schreibaufgabe vor: Neo (Thomas Anderson), der zumindest noch in dieser Sequenz von der Existenz der Matrix nicht überzeugt ist, schreibt über seine Erfahrungen einen fesselnden Bericht für ein Internetportal. Für solche Berichte sind zunächst fünf Leitfragen zu beantworten, was auch anzeigt, inwiefern dieser Teil des Films von der Lerngruppe verstanden wurde:

> Who is the report about?
> What happened to the person?
> When did it happen?
> Where did it happen?
> Why and how did it happen?

Wir schlagen vor, dass die Schülerinnen und Schüler diese Fragen zunächst in Kleingruppen stichpunktartig beantworten und anschließend ihre Notizen mit denen einer anderen Schülergruppe austauschen, um eventuell weitere (spannende) Details zu ergänzen und ihren Wortschatz zu erweitern, bevor die Berichte auf der Grundlage der Notizen individuell geschrieben werden (Hausaufgabe).

4.3 Bonfire: Margaret Atwood, *Oryx and Crake*

Während Atwoods *The Handmaid's Tale* eine politische Dystopie genannt werden kann und damit klar in der Orwell'schen Tradition steht, geht es in *Oryx and Crake* um die Selbstvernichtung der Menschheit durch hemmungslose Forschung und die Profitgier alles beherrschender Gentechnologie-Unternehmen, die weltweite Pandemien zur Folge hat. Die Aktualität dieses Exzerptes ist zum jetzigen Zeitpunkt noch gar nicht absehbar. Am 9.5.2006 lief im US-Fernsehsender ABC der Film *Fatal Contact: Bird Flu in America*. Mehrere hundert Millionen Menschen fallen dort dem mutierten Virus zum Opfer, die Weltwirtschaft kollabiert und nichts kann dagegen getan werden.[1]

Im Romanauszug treffen wir zunächst auf den einsamen, halb verhungerten und halb wahnsinnigen Protagonisten, Snowman, der einem gewissen Crake die Schuld für sein Dilemma gibt. Im Folgenden erfährt der Leser, dass Wissenschaftler neue Tierarten gezüchtet haben, z. B. als (unfreiwillige) Organspender für menschliche Patienten. Als aufgrund ökologischer Katastrophen Fleisch immer seltener wurde, dienten diese neuen Tiere zunehmend auch als Nahrung. Inwieweit dieses für die Ausrottung der Menschheit mitverantwortlich war, bleibt zunächst noch unklar.

Für diese Zeitebene verwendet Atwood das Präsens, für den folgenden Abschnitt, in dem Snowman, der in seinem früheren Leben Jimmy hieß, sich an ein frühes Kindheitserlebnis erinnert, das Präteritum. Damals besuchte er mit seinem Vater ein „Freudenfeuer", dass in Wirklichkeit der Vernichtung großer Mengen von Nutztieren diente, die an einer Tierseuche gestorben waren. Die anwesenden Erwachsenen vermuteten, dass die Krankheitserreger absichtlich gezüchtet worden waren, um die Fleischpreise in die Höhe zu treiben. Korruption soll die Aufdeckung des Verbrechens verhindert haben.

Wir schlagen folgende *pre-reading activity* vor:

Sie teilen die Kursteilnehmerinnen und Kursteilnehmer in zwei Gruppen, A und B, ein und lassen zunächst jede(n) alleine etwa drei Minuten für sich die folgenden Fragen beantworten (Stichpunkte notieren lassen).

Group A: How would you spend your day alone on a tropical island?

Group B: What would you miss if you had to spend your day alone on a tropical Island?

Die Schülerinnen und Schüler bilden danach, wie im ersten Kapitel beschrieben, einen Doppelkreis und informieren sich gegenseitig über ihre Überlegungen.

Danach wird im Plenum an der Tafel gesammelt, was die Schülerinnen und Schüler im Gespräch erfahren haben; es sollten also jeweils die Zuhörer das nennen, was sie von ihren Mitschülerinnen und Mitschülern gehört haben. Clustern Sie die Ergebnisse, ordnen Sie also ähnliche Punkte einander zu bzw. lassen Sie Schülerinnen und Schüler dieses tun. Dies kann mit farbigen Papierstreifen geschehen, auf die die jeweiligen Zuhörer die genannten Punkte geschrieben haben, die dann mit Magneten an der Tafel befestigt werden; es kann aber natürlich auch einfach an die Tafel geschrieben werden.

Wahrscheinlich werden die Erwartungen an einen Tag auf einer tropischen Insel utopische Züge tragen, wenngleich vermutlich z. B. PC, Gamecube, MP3-Player, DVD, Shopping, Gespräche mit Freunden, Schmusen mit Freund/Freundin vermisst werden.

Bei der anschließenden Lektüre wird den Schülerinnen und Schülern schnell klar werden, dass Jimmy im Gegensatz zum Ergebnis der *pre-reading activity* sein Leben als alles andere

[1] Mehr Informationen, einschließlich kritischer Stimmen, zu dem Film finden Sie hier: http://www.nytimes.com/2006/05/09/arts/television/09stan.html?_r=1&th&emc=th&oref=slogin

als ideal empfindet, wir es also nicht mit einer Utopie, sondern mit einer Dystopie zu tun haben.
Im anschließenden Unterrichtsgespräch sollten außer den *while-reading questions* die folgenden drei Aspekte angesprochen werden:

1. "Sometimes he laughs like a hyena or roars like a lion – his idea of a hyena, his idea of a lion." (p. 63, ll. 7f.). Explain the difference between laughing like a hyena and the idea of a hyena.

   Probably there are no hyenas anymore. Like most species, including human beings, they have become extinct. It seems that only pigoons and wolvogs have survived (and perhaps other animals created in gene-labs) since they are better adapted to the new environmental conditions.

2. Considering the long annotation on p. 63 of the textbook: What might be the reason for Snowman's loneliness?

   On the one hand, ecological disasters due to mankind's environmental arrogance (radiation holes in the atmosphere, melting of the polar ice caps, flooding of coastal cities, drought, desertification of the continents); on the other hand, boundless profit seeking that caused people to sell the meat of genetically created animals that were supposed to be used for medical purposes only.[1]

3. What effect does the chosen point of view of this extract have on the reader?

   Limited point of view, third-person narrative (in the first part about a grown-up man, in the second about the same person when he was a young boy). The narrator is an anonymous person who tells us about the events and characters and often includes Jimmy's thoughts and feelings (e.g. p. 63, ll. 8–12; p. 64, ll. 1 ff.). Particularly in the touching second part the reader is enabled to identify with little Jimmy when he was afraid that the "bonfire" might hurt the animals.

Nun bietet sich auch ein kurzer kontrastierender Vergleich der Ergebnisse der *pre-reading activity* mit Snowman's Gegenwart an.
Da der folgende Text demselben Roman entnommen wurde und manche noch offene Frage klären wird, empfehlen wir ein zügiges Voranschreiten zum nächsten Exzerpt. Im Idealfall lassen Sie Ihre Schülerinnen und Schüler den zweiten *Oryx and Crake*-Auszug daheim lesen und die *while-reading questions* schriftlich beantworten.

[1] Hier könnte sich eine Diskussion zu dem Thema anschließen, inwiefern man hier überhaupt noch von *Science Fiction* reden kann bzw. wie weit das von Atwood entworfene Horrorszenario zumindest teilweise bereits Realität geworden ist.

4.4 Paradice project: Margaret Atwood, *Oryx and Crake*

In diesem Teil erinnert sich Jimmy wieder an ein wichtiges Erlebnis in seiner Vergangenheit, folglich verwendet Atwood hier das Präteritum.
Lassen Sie Ihre Schülerinnen und Schüler zunächst über Sinn und Bedeutung der Kapitelüberschrift spekulieren. Eventuell werden Sie sie auf die abweichende Schreibweise von *paradise* hinweisen müssen.

What do you associate with "paradice"?
Paradise: happy, peaceful life of plenty
dice: gambling, coincidence, chance, things might get out of hand

Tatsächlich ist es Jimmys früherem Freund, dem genialen jungen Wissenschaftler Crake, gelungen, eine neue menschliche Spezies und einen für sie perfekten künstlichen Lebensraum zu erschaffen. Die *Crakers* sind individuell gestaltete, gutmütige, wunderschöne menschliche Wesen aller Hautfarben, mit einem verbesserten Immunsystem und einer UV-resistenten Haut, die baldmöglichst in den Verkauf gehen und großen Profit bringen sollen. Die *Crakers* kennen weder Hierarchien und (rassistische) Vorurteile noch Ehrgeiz oder Eifersucht und können, wenn nötig, von ihren eigenen Exkrementen leben. Sie alleine haben, mit Ausnahme von Jimmy, die Katastrophe überlebt, so einen Neuanfang der Menschheit ermöglicht und erst damit Crake zum wahren Schöpfer gemacht (Oryx war die einzige Frau, die Jimmy jemals liebte. Er meint bisweilen noch immer ihre Stimme zu hören, obgleich auch sie den Kataklysmus nicht überlebt hat, und präsentiert sie den kindlich-naiven *Crakers* als Schöpfergöttin neben Crake – daher der Titel *Oryx and Crake).*
Nach Besprechung der *while-reading questions* empfiehlt sich – im Plenum – ein Vergleich zwischen *Crakers* und den Menschen in *Brave New World.* Die Ergebnisse sollten an der Tafel festgehalten werden.

Point out parallels and differences between the Crakers and people in *Brave New World.*

Differences		**Parallels**
Brave New World	*Oryx and Crake*	
• individual conditioning for Alphas, Betas etc. • consumption- and sex-orientated • …	• all share the same character traits • childish, naïve, satisfied with what they have • …	• created by genetic engineering • perfectly "adapted" to their environment • die comparatively young without ever experiencing old age • …

Äußerlich und charakterlich sind die *Crakers* wahrscheinlich am ehesten mit Well's *Eloi* zu vergleichen.
Auch die folgende Kreativaufgabe dient u. a. dazu, das vertiefte Textverständnis zu überprüfen.
Die Schülerinnen und Schüler sollen zunächst in Gruppen (Mindeststärke vier) die folgende Szene vorbereiten (20–30 Minuten) und anschließend vorspielen:

Playwriting and acting: Meeting the Crakers

Choose two present-day time travellers who arrive in the year 2244. In the meantime, mankind has destroyed itself. Only a small group of humanoids, who call themselves the Crakers (and normally run around naked but may stay dressed for this particular scene), have survived. They look very much like you and even speak English, yet their behaviour is very weird in your eyes. Write – and later act – the scene (keywords are sufficient for your preparation).

Preliminary considerations:

- What are the Crakers doing when the time travellers meet them?
- How will they react when they see other human beings, who have arrived in a strange machine? Take into consideration their character traits, which are in their genes and therefore unalterable.
- How will the time travellers treat them?
- What will they talk about?
- Will the time travellers decide to stay or to return? Why?

Wir empfehlen, die Szenen mit einer Videokamera aufzunehmen. Sollten Sie (oder Ihre Schule) keine Videokamera besitzen, bitten Sie einfach einen Schüler oder eine Schülerin in der Stunde zuvor, eine eigene von daheim mitzubringen. Auch wenn sich Ihre Kursteilnehmer zunächst (scheinbar) gegen eine Aufnahme sträuben, hat eine laufende Kamera doch immer einen enorm anspornenden Effekt. Die Schülerinnen und Schüler legen sich einfach viel mehr ins Zeug, simulieren Neugier, Tränen, Wut, Angst und andere Gefühle auf zum Teil höchst überzeugende Weise. Außerdem lassen sich die Ergebnisse nach einem anschließenden Vorspielen der Kassette noch besser vergleichen.
Gute Erfahrungen haben wir auch mit der folgenden Bewertungspraxis gemacht:
Nach dem Vorspielen jeder Szene bewerten die jeweils anderen Gruppen die Leistung mit Punkten (z. B. „1“: poor, „2“: acceptable, „3“: good, „4“: outstanding). Dafür sollten vorher einige Kriterien genannt oder gemeinsam festgelegt werden (z. B. Ideenreichtum/schauspielerische Leistung/Plausibilität/...). Die Gruppe, die zum Schluss die meisten Punkte gesammelt hat, kann einen Preis erhalten (z. B. eine gute Note oder eine Nascherei).

Als Hausaufgabe zur nächsten Stunde empfehlen wir das Lesen des folgenden Textes nebst schriftlicher Beantwortung der *while-reading questions.*

4.5 The dimples of DelGlacey: M. T. Anderson, *Feed*

Mit Violet hat M. T. Anderson eine Figur geschaffen, die aus vielen klassischen Dystopien bekannt ist – die des Dissidenten bzw. in diesem Fall die der Dissidentin. Da jedoch in dem Exzerpt aus *Brave New World* der *Savage* nicht vorkommt und auch Winston in dem *1984*-Auszug noch nicht weiter als Regimegegner in Erscheinung getreten ist, kann hier kein Vergleich vorgenommen werden (es sei denn, Schülerinnen oder Schüler berichten in Referaten über die Inhalte der ganzen Romane). In jedem Fall aber sollte der Unterschied zwischen Titus' *Feed*-beschränktem Denken und Reden einerseits und Violets kritischerer Intelligenz andererseits erarbeitet werden. Die zweite und dritte *while-reading question* bereiten darauf vor. Wir empfehlen, die Ergebnisse der drei Fragen an der Tafel zu sammeln, z. B. mithilfe zweier Tabellen, da diese den Schülerinnen und Schülern bei der folgenden Kreativaufgabe hilfreich sein werden.

School in the past	School™
run by the government …	run by influential corporations …

(weitere Punkte siehe „Musterantworten“, S. 91)

Titus	Violet
totally dependent on his Feed …	smarter than Titus, thinks more independently …

(weitere Punkte siehe „Musterantworten“, S. 91)

Der erste Teil des Textes beschäftigt sich vor allem mit dem Thema *education*, der zweite mit Chancen und Gefahren der Gentechnologie.
Für den ersten Teil empfehlen wir, nach Klärung inhaltlicher Aspekte mithilfe der *while-reading questions,* die folgenden Kreativaufgaben.
Die meisten Kursteilnehmer beschäftigen sich in Gruppen von drei oder vier Mitgliedern mit folgendem Thema:

Titus and his friends are on their way to the latest "supersize" mall. What information do their Feeds send them? Choose one student who will have to act Titus or one of his (male or female) friends, discuss the Feed's messages and decide on where to go and what to do first …

Drei oder vier von Ihnen ausgewählte Schülerinnen oder Schüler sollen später die Rolle der Violet übernehmen. Eine überdurchschnittliche sprachliche Kompetenz und ein kritischer Geist sind dafür sicher hilfreich. Während die anderen die eben genannten Aufgaben bearbeiten, bereitet sich die „Violet-Gruppe“ auf Folgendes vor:

You are Violet. Together with Titus and some friends, you are on the way to a new mall. Your Feeds are sending you masses of information about the latest fashion and what to buy. Your companions are rapt, yet you remain calm and keep a critical distance. What will you say and do when the others begin to exchange their new knowledge about the latest must-haves? Choose one student from your group to play Violet.

Vorbereitungszeit: ca. 10 Minuten; Dauer des Rollenspiels: solange sich die Schülerinnen und Schüler etwas zu sagen haben (wahrscheinlich nicht länger als 5 Minuten).

Zur Arbeit mit dem zweiten Teil des Auszugs aus *Feed* (ab S. 73, Z. 13) empfehlen wir, zunächst folgende Frage beantworten zu lassen:

What do we learn about how Titus was conceived?

His mum says to him: "You're just the boy we wanted. […] You're just what we asked for" (p. 74, ll. 7f.). In the following section, we learn that he was genetically engineered to have his father's eyes and mouth and his mother's hands and nose. The parents seem to be particularly proud of having chosen for him "the chins, dimples, and hairline of DelGlacey Murdoch" (p. 74, ll. 16f.), who they considered to be the most handsome actor of his time. After watching DelGlacey in a movie, they went to a place called a *conceptionarium* (p. 74, l. 31), where they probably donated sperm and egg cells and left all the rest to the geneticists working there.

Als Hausaufgabe zur nächsten Stunde sollte *Copy 11* gelesen und die dort zu findenden Aufgaben bearbeitet werden. Nachdem in den Auszügen aus *Brave New World, Oryx and Crake* und *Feed* viel von In-Vitro-Befruchtung, künstlich herbeigeführten genetischen Veränderungen, Produktion von Wunschkindern etc. die Rede war, scheint es uns an der Zeit zu sein, den Stand der gegenwärtigen Forschung mit der *Science Fiction*-Literatur zu vergleichen. Der ausgewählte Artikel ist zwar schon ein paar Jahre alt, hat aber, da er sich vor allem mit der Zukunft der Gentechnologie beschäftigt, nichts von seiner Aktualität eingebüßt. Die lockere, z.T. humorvolle Art und Weise, wie der Autor mit dem Thema umgeht und wie es ihm gelingt, schwierige Sachverhalte auch Laien verständlich zu machen, haben uns diesen Text besonders geeignet erscheinen lassen.

Lösungsvorschläge zu *Copy 11*:

1. Healthier, more intelligent, talented and attractive children will be born.
2. A lot can be done with the DNA of animals already. Scientists are convinced that the considerable breakthroughs in genetically-engineered lab mice and farm animals will soon be applied to human beings. "It's not a question of 'if' but 'when' and 'how' this will occur" (l. 26). For example, it has been possible to dial in a higher amount of good cholesterol in mice, which reduces the risk of heart diseases immensely. In addition, higher intelligence in mice can already be achieved through genetic engineering.
   The article does not withhold from the readers that technical obstacles will have to be overcome if successes like these are to be transferred to human beings.
3. - informal words and expressions: "kids" (l. 5), "stuff" (l. 72), "big ticket illnesses (l. 48), "gene-shopping parents" (l. 60)
   - incomplete or broken sentence constructions: "Sound pretty good?" (l. 3), more examples in ll. 2, 33, 37, 63f.
   - author repeatedly addresses the reader: "your answer" (l. 9), "you" (l. 55)
   - imperatives: "Suppose" (ll. 1, 4, 5), "Insert a block" (l. 33)

   Aim: to make compact information, such as in ll. 51ff. and 61ff., more digestible and the article as a whole more enjoyable. In this respect, it can be considered to be a good example of popular science writing.

Abschließend kann – zum Glück – festgestellt werden, dass die In-vitro-Genese eines Titus, wenn überhaupt, eben doch erst in ferner Zukunft möglich sein wird.
Lassen Sie Ihre Schülerinnen und Schüler daheim die folgende Kurzgeschichte in Kombination mit *Copy 12,* Aufgaben 1 bis 5, lesen. (Die Fragen 1, 2, 7 und 8 auf dem Arbeitsblatt wiederholen im Übrigen Erkenntnisse, die im Laufe dieser Einheit gewonnen werden sollten.)

Designer babies

Suppose parents-to-be could guarantee their children will grow up to be unusually healthy. Or extra smart. Or maybe just a little better looking than mom and dad. Sound pretty good?

Now, suppose that guarantee requires a level of planning that goes way beyond the usual prenatal care. Suppose it requires some fiddling with the future kids' DNA, adding a few genes here and there to slow down aging or rev up the brain circuitry or lock in resistance to viruses.

Still sound good?

Even if your answer is a definite no, some scientists believe many parents will find this a very attractive option. For now, the choice is science fiction – but just barely so. The time is coming, many scientists say, when parents will pick their children's genes.

From the menu of possibilities, parents might select genes to make their babies resist common diseases and infections, things like cancer, AIDS, heart attacks and Alzheimer's disease. Maybe they would like their children to have fabulous memories or winning personalities or a talent for playing the piano.

A couple of extra inches of height and a thick head of hair could be nice, too.

To hear these scientists talk, all of this and much more will be possible in the not-so-distant future. "There's nothing beyond tinkering," says Lee Silver, a Princeton biologist.

Not this year or next, probably, and maybe not in the next 10 or even 20 years. But these scientists predict the amazing breakthroughs in genetically engineering lab mice and farm critters will eventually be applied to the animals at the top of the food chain.

Us.

"It's not a question of 'if' but 'when' and 'how' this will occur," says Gregory Stock, head of the Program on Medicine, Technology and Society at UCLA's School of Medicine.

Stock and Silver are visionaries in their field, men who enjoy painting the big picture of an over-the-horizon science called human germline engineering. Germline refers to the sperm and egg. These scientists are talking about changing the genetic makeup of a person-to-be at the moment of conception.

Something like this: Insert a block of new genes into a freshly fertilized egg. The one cell becomes two, then four, then eight. Each new version carries the extra information. In nine months, a baby is born. Every cell in his or her body contains the extra genes.

The child grows up. Marries. Passes the extra genes on to the next generation of babies. And they on to theirs. And so on. Or maybe not. The unsettling prospect of handing these genetic fixes down the generations is just one of the many controversies of this obviously hot-button field.

"The reason people are fascinated by this whole area is that it will challenge our fundamental thinking about who we are and what it means to be human," says Stock. "We are talking about remaking human biology."

But what part of biology to remake first? Typically the answer is to reduce our tendency to get sick.

While personal habits and medical care play an obvious role in health, inheriting good genes gives some folks a powerful edge. Scientists already know some of the combinations of genes that help people resist some big-ticket illnesses. So one goal of human germline engineering could be to help the genetically less fortunate share these built-in health advantages.

For instance, the risk of heart disease depends in part on the levels of HDL, the good cholesterol. More is clearly better. In the human body, a gene called apO-A1 makes a

prenatal prior to childbirth
to rev up to speed up, improve
to tinker *etwa: herumbasteln*
person-to-be sb yet unborn
unsettling disturbing, causing worry
hot-button stirring up strong feelings
edge here: advantage

major piece of HDL. The same is true in mice, whose biology, scientists love to point out, is not so different from ours.

"It's possible in mice to dial in virtually any HDL level you want by introducing more copies of this gene," says Dr. R. Sanders Williams, a cardiologist at the University of Texas Southwestern Medical Center.

So why not add some extra apO-A1 genes to one-cell persons-to-be and reduce their chance of dying from humanity's leading killer? Perhaps resistance to the AIDS virus would also appeal to gene-shopping parents. Scientists can imagine a way to do that. Those who are born with two defective copies of a gene called CCR5 can escape HIV infection despite thousands or risky sexual encounters. The reason: CCR5 makes a protein that the AIDS virus locks onto when it invades white blood cells. So, no CCR5 protein on the surface of a cell – no infection.

Of course, there is no reason to stop with disease protection, the visionaries say. Many genetic "enhancements," as they are called, can also be imagined.

One obvious enhancement is extra brain power. At Princeton, scientists have already created mice – nicknamed "Doogie" after TV's physician prodigy – that are rodent geniuses. They learn faster, remember longer and adapt to changes better than any ordinary mouse.

What makes these mice unique is an extra copy of a gene that produces a brain chemical called NR2B. This stuff boosts the cellular switches that help the brain store associations. (When you remember the name that goes with a face, that's an association.) While a human brain is more complex than a mouse's, the basic machinery of learning may be pretty much the same in both. Even selecting a child's personality in advance might be possible. Experts believe that half of people's personality traits are hard-wired by their genes. Of course, lots of genes combine to create any individual's melange of quirks and temperament. So building a child with, say, David Letterman wit, Mother Theresa compassion and Warren Buffett business sense may not be real easy at first. [...]

Eventually, the thinking goes, scientists will figure out which genes bestow prized talents and characteristics. These, too, could go on the menu of genetic possibilities browsed by parents who are designing their babies.

But this idea brings up just one of a very long list of technical obstacles. Everyone reading this article already owns two copies of every standard-issue gene. In most cases, just dropping in another really good one is unlikely to do much. So engineers will have to figure out some way to reliably shut down the existing so-so genes so the supergenes can take over. The field's visionaries toss off sweep-of-the-hand solutions for this and many other problems and predict the science fiction will become science within a generation.

"I think it could occur 10 years from whenever we decide it should," says John Campbell, a UCLA neurobiologist. "It depends a lot on motivation. It won't be limited by science." [...]

by Daniel Q. Haney, AP Medical Editor; http://www.netlink.de/gen/Zeitung/2000/000305.html;

enhancement improvement
prodigy person with exceptional intelligence or talent

switch exchange, transfer

hard-wired here: pre-determined and fixed in the brain
melange mixture, blend
quirk strange habit, eccentricity
David Letterman famous US talk show host; in Germany copied by Harald Schmidt
Mother Theresa founder of "The Missionaries of Charity" in Calcutta, was awarded The Nobel Peace Prize in 1979
Warren Buffett very successful US stock market tycoon
toss off sweep-of-the-hand throw in quick and seemingly easy

1. Which advantages of changing unborn children's DNA are mentioned in the text?
2. What has been achieved already? What is still science fiction?
3. Mark colloquial and informal words and expressions. Why do you think the author has made use of them?

4.6 I love my wife: Robert Sheckley, *The Perfect Woman*

Der letzte Prosatext der Textausgabe ist gleichzeitig die einzige Kurzgeschichte, die wir ausgewählt haben. Obgleich es sich um den ältesten der sechs Texte dieses Kapitels handelt, haben wir ihn ans Ende gesetzt, da uns seine humorvolle Note ein besserer Abschluss zu sein schien als die doch zum Teil recht pessimistischen oder gar beängstigenden Romanauszüge zuvor. Die Ähnlichkeit der Genese von Myra, der Titelfigur in *The Perfect Woman*, und von Titus im vorherigen Auszug kann eine gute Überleitung darstellen.
Wir empfehlen, bei der Analyse der Kurzgeschichte relativ zügig vorzugehen, da die anschließende Kreativaufgabe, die den Schülerinnen und Schülern erfahrungsgemäß sehr viel Spaß macht, auch die Inhalte und das Verständnis überprüfen wird.

Lösungsvorschläge zu *Copy 12*:

1. **Author-coined vocabulary** to create an other-worldly atmosphere: "Triad-Morgan party", "Primitivist", "Primitive Woman", "Thank Stat", "celebration points", "Seffiners", "Modern Woman". **Non-existing technology:** androids that look exactly like human beings, speaking cars, etc.
2. "All Earth" celebrating together, "Peace and prosperity to all". The idea of artificially-produced house- and/or sex slaves is certainly terrifying for most people.
3. Buttering too much toast for Morcheck (p. 77, ll. 3–5); kissing him on the nose instead of his bald spot (p. 77, ll. 5f.); being unable to cope with his questions (p. 77, ll. 30–37)
4. "She needed a checkup." (p. 77, l. 40)
5. "**back** to the factory" (p. 78, l. 38)

Anschließend sollten im Plenum die noch ausstehenden Aufgaben 6 bis 8 bearbeitet werden.

6.

Modern Women	Primitive Women
• androids looking like women/ housewives	• female human beings with virtues and vices
• entirely devoted to the well-being of their husbands	• have proved their equality and taken over some men's jobs
• probably built and programmed according to their (future) husbands' wishes	• nevertheless , fulfil female stereotypes (e.g. expect money for clothes, talk for hours on the telephone)

7. Myra is an android whereas the Crakers are a new species of artificially-created human beings. Both are designed according to their later buyers' wishes.
(Hier könnte auch, falls noch nicht geschehen, ein Vergleich zu Titus Genese in *Feed* gezogen werden, dessen Äußeres auch exakt gemäß den Wünschen seiner Eltern konzipiert wurde.)
8. Particularly the last lines (the speaking car with its conventional replies) cannot be taken seriously. Moreover, there are some weird improbabilities: the advanced technology of the year 3000 is capable of producing (almost) perfect androids, but no dishwashers. The enumera-

Robert Sheckley, *The Perfect Woman*

1. Mark (or copy) all elements of the short story that show you that this is science fiction.

2. Which utopian ideas can be found in the first paragraph? Are there also dystopian elements in the story?

3. When does the reader get the feeling that Myra is not well?

4. At which moment does it become clear what Modern Women like Myra really are?

5. The last line contains a word which might be regarded to be the clue to the story. Which word is it?

6. Collect all characteristics of Modern and Primitive Women.

Modern Women	Primitive Women

7. What's the essential difference between Modern Women and the Crakers in *Oryx and Crake?*

8. This is, of course, a science-fiction story. Yet it is not a very serious example of the genre. Where does it become clear that Sheckley does not take the matter too seriously?

tion of Primitive Women's habits and characteristics on p. 77, ll. 13–20 is so full of misogynistic stereotypes that it can only be taken as a joke.

Sollte dieses eine Einzelstunde sein, empfehlen wir, bereits jetzt die folgenden *role-play cards* auszugeben, damit sich die Schülerinnen und Schüler daheim in Ruhe auf ihre Rollen vorbereiten können. Ansonsten muss die Vorbereitung auf das *phone in* in einer kurzen Stillarbeitsphase im Unterricht geschehen. Da Sie wahrscheinlich mehr Kursteilnehmer als Rollen haben, müssen einige doppelt besetzt werden (z. B. die der anrufenden Unterstützer der Protagonisten). Bei sehr großen Kursen bilden die Schülerinnen und Schüler Gruppen, die zunächst Argumente sammeln und dann ein oder zwei Gruppenmitglieder bestimmen, die dann die jeweiligen Rollen ausfüllen.

Phone in: Man 3000

Mithilfe von *role-play cards* (siehe Hinweise auf den folgenden Seiten) wird eine Radio-Talkshow erarbeitet und durchgespielt, in deren Verlauf *Modernists* und *Primitivists* zu Wort kommen. Sie sollen ihre Argumente darlegen und miteinander diskutieren. Auf ihre Äußerungen hin rufen Zuhörer an, die klar auf der Seite von Morcheck oder Owen-Clark stehen oder aber mit Ratschlägen zwischen den beiden vermitteln wollen. Das Ende der Diskussion ist – im Gegensatz zu der selbstgeschriebenen Szene zu *Oryx and Crake* – offen und hängt völlig von der Argumentationskraft und dem Einfallsreichtum der Darbietenden ab. Die Rolle des Moderators ist in diesem Fall entscheidend und sollte von einer dazu fähigen Schülerin oder einem entsprechend begabten Schüler ausgeübt werden. Diese/r kann allen Teilnehmern z. B. auch dadurch eine Denkpause einräumen, dass sie/er (ähnlich wie in einer realen Radio-Talkshow) kurz ein Musikstück einspielt, nach dem der Austausch der Argumente fortgesetzt wird.
Je nach Kreativität und Lebendigkeit des Kurses sind zwischen 20 und 30 Minuten für das *phone in* zu veranschlagen. Wir haben dabei auch schon Videokameras oder Tonbandgeräte eingesetzt.
Als kreative Hausaufgabe können Sie Ihre Schülerinnen und Schüler abschließend über *„My life with a modern partner"* schreiben lassen.

Im Film *Stepford Wives* geht es um das gleiche Thema: Männer haben sich künstliche Frauen geschaffen, die ihnen das Leben angenehm und bequem machen sollen. Es gibt zwei Versionen, eine von 1978, u. a. mit Katharine Ross und Patrick O'Neal und eine neuere von 2004 mit Nicole Kidman, Matthew Broderick, Bette Midler und Glenn Close. Wir halten beide für empfehlenswert, die zweite besonders aufgrund der Schauspielerinnen und Schauspieler, die den Schülerinnen und Schülern bekannt sein dürften, die erste, da sie die dystopischen und Science Fiction-Elemente stärker in den Mittelpunkt des Geschehens stellt.

Before the program: You are the **radio-host of the popular phone-in program "Man 3000".** People call you to talk about their problems and share their personal stories with you and your listeners. Tonight a serious issue is to be discussed: "Should Men choose Modern or Primitive Wives?" You'll have two guests, Mr. Owen-Clark, who is a Primitivist, and Mr. Morcheck, whose beloved Modern Wife, Myra, had to be taken back to the factory due to malfunction. Prepare the questions you want to ask them in order to find out why they prefer a Primitive or Modern Woman.
During the program, it will also be part of your task to have your callers introduce themselves, to question them about their opinion and feelings on the matter and to encourage other listeners to phone-in to the program and share their thoughts.
You will have a psychologist as an expert on the topic at your side in the studio.

Appoint someone from your group who will play the host during the program.

Before the popular phone-in program "Man 3000": You are **Mr. Morcheck.** The loss of Myra in combination with your colleague Owen-Clark's gloating is driving you crazy and you don't know what to do about it. Be prepared to tell the presenter and the listeners what is making you so unhappy and why you prefer Modern to Primitive Women. Moreover, be prepared for some VERY personal questions from the host!
During the program, you will hear Owen-Clark's position, too. You will also listen to people who either support you or Owen-Clark or who would like to help the two of you find a solution to your conflict. Listen carefully to the other phone-in participants and interact with them.

Appoint someone from your group who will play Mr. Morcheck during the program.

Before the popular phone-in program "Man 3000": You are **Mr. Owen-Clark,** a Primitivist who cannot understand why your colleague Morcheck prefers Modern Women. Be prepared to tell the presenter and the listeners what you like in Primitive and despise in Modern Women. Be prepared for some VERY personal questions from the host!
During the program, you will hear Morcheck's position, too. You will also listen to people who either support you or him or who would like to help the two of you find a solution to your conflict. Listen carefully to the other phone-in participants and interact with them.

Appoint someone from your group who will play Mr. Owen-Clark during the program.

Before the popular phone-in program "Man 3000": You, a **Modern Woman,** as well as **a listener and caller.** You fully understand Mr. Morcheck's position and you want to support him in this discussion by telling the participants and other listeners your point of view.
Before the program, prepare what you are going to tell the presenter and listeners, e.g. the great advantages of Modern Women over Primitive ones.
During the program, listen carefully to the opponents' explanations first and then present your arguments to the best effect.

Appoint two people from your group who will play Modern Women.

Before the popular phone-in program "Man 3000": You, a **Primitive Woman,** as well as **a listener and caller.** You fully understand Mr. Owen-Clark's position and you want to support him in this discussion by telling the participants and other listeners your point of view.
Before the program, prepare what you are going to tell the presenter and listeners, e.g. the great advantages of Primitive Women over Modern ones.
During the program, listen carefully to the opponents' explanations first and then present your arguments to the best effect.

Appoint two people from your group who will play Primitive Women.

Before the popular phone-in program "Man 3000": You are a **psychologist** and an expert on the advantages and disadvantages of having a Modern Wife.
Before the program, recall what you know about Modern and Primitive Women and what living with them means to their husbands.
During the program, listen to the participants' argumentation and – when asked by the presenter – try to react in a constructive and helpful manner.

Appoint someone from your group who will play the psychologist during the program.

Before the popular phone-in program "Man 3000": You, **the husband of a Primitive Woman,** are **a listener and caller.** You fully understand Mr. Owen-Clark's position and you want to support him in this discussion by telling the participants and other listeners your point of view.
Before the program, prepare what you are going to tell the presenter and listeners, e.g. the great advantages of Primitive Women over Modern ones.
During the program, listen carefully to the opponents' explanations first and then present your arguments to the best effect.

Appoint two people from your group who will play husbands of Primitive Women.

Before the popular phone-in program "Man 3000": You, **the husband of a Modern Woman,** are **a listener and caller.** You fully understand Mr. Morcheck's position and you want to support him in this discussion by telling the participants and other listeners your point of view.
Before the program, prepare what you are going to tell the presenter and listeners, e.g. the great advantages of Modern Women over Primitive ones.
During the program, listen carefully to the opponents' explanations first and then present your arguments to the best effect.

Appoint two people from your group who will play husbands of Modern Women.

Before the popular phone-in program "Man 3000": You, **the owner of a factory producing Modern Women,** are **a listener and caller.** You fully understand Mr. Morcheck's position and you want to support him in this discussion by telling the participants and other listeners your point of view.
Before the program, prepare what you are going to tell the presenter and listeners, e.g. the great advantages of Modern Women over Primitive ones.
During the program, listen carefully to the opponents' explanations first and then present your arguments to the best effect.

Appoint someone from your group who will play this factory owner.

Component 5

Utopia or dystopia in poetry and song

Wir empfehlen, die Präsentation der Songs überwiegend Schülerinnen und Schüler übernehmen zu lassen (natürlich auch von nicht in der Textausgabe abgedruckten, aber thematisch geeigneten anderen Liedern). Ihren Schülerinnen und Schülern sollte es in der Regel nicht schwerfallen, sich Aufnahmen der Songs zu beschaffen – wenn sie sie nicht ohnehin schon besitzen. Die meisten von uns ausgewählten Texte eignen sich auch für Hörverstehensübungen (z. B. mithilfe eines Lückentextes). Im Zentrum der Diskussion sollten allerdings stets die darin enthaltenen utopischen oder dystopischen Elemente stehen.
Exemplarisch wird im Folgenden der anspruchsvolle REM-Song behandelt.

5.1 It starts with an earthquake: REM, *It's the End of the World (As We Know it)*

REM produziert seit den 1980er-Jahren und gehört unbestreitbar zu den erfolgreichsten Rockbands weltweit. Anders als andere Bands, die schnell wieder verschwunden sind, haben REM einen langsamen, aber stetigen Aufstieg geschafft und viele andere Bands mit ihrer Musik inspiriert. Seit Ende der 80er-Jahre verarbeiten REM in ihrer Musik vor allem aktuelle politische, soziale und ökologische Themen, die Bands, die ein Massenpublikum anziehen, sonst eher selten aufgreifen. Mit dem hier ausgewählten Lied ist REM ein ironisch-apokalyptischer Titel gelungen, in dem die Musiker ein eher düsteres Zukunftsszenario beschreiben.
Bei der inhaltlichen wie auch bei der musikalischen Interpretation des Liedes können verschiedene Ansätze zum Tragen kommen: Auffällig ist der schnelle, hektische Rhythmus des Stückes; in weiten Teilen handelt es sich um einen Sprechgesang. Der temporeiche Gesang lässt auf eine öffentliche Debatte schließen *(policy debate)* – eine Form der ursprünglich an Colleges praktizierten Form der Auseinandersetzung, in der die Sprecher möglichst schnell sprechen, um möglichst viele Argumente innerhalb einer engen Zeitbegrenzung nennen zu können. Bandleader Michael Stipe soll während der Entstehungszeit des Songs tatsächlich einen Freund, der in einem öffentlichen Debattierwettbewerb vortrug, besucht haben.
Daneben sind in einzelnen Textpassagen Nachrichtenmeldungen verarbeitet; diese werden allerdings ungeordnet bzw. kaum strukturiert wiedergegeben und von *comic reliefs* unterbrochen. Auch ein Traum Stipes soll im Lied verarbeitet worden sein, in dem er Gast einer Geburtstagsfeier gewesen sein soll, deren Gäste alle die Initialen „L. B." hatten. In einem Interview sagte der Sänger, dass apokalyptische Bilder durchaus auch Gegenstand seiner Träume seien.
It's the End of the World hat die Struktur eines inneren Monologs *(stream of consciousness),* worauf neben der inhaltlichen Struktur des Titels auch formale Merkmale wie das Fehlen von Satzzeichen und andere Regelverstöße hindeuten.
Der Versuch, eine widerspruchsfreie Interpretation zu liefern, wird voraussichtlich scheitern. Vielmehr sind unterschiedliche Deutungen denkbar und vor dem Entstehungshintergrund auch legitim. Erschwerend kommt hinzu, dass an keiner Stelle Bezüge zu konkreten Akteuren oder Lokalitäten (was auch charakteristisch für Träume sein kann) deutlich werden, wenn man von Lenny Bruce, Leonid Brezhnev und Lester Bangs absieht. Einerseits stehen

diese stellvertretend für die Gäste in Stipes Traum, andererseits könnten sie auch stellvertretend für die Konfrontation der Blöcke (Kalter Krieg) vor 1989 stehen, was für die Interpretation des Liedinhalts ein hilfreicher Ansatzpunkt wäre. Letztlich besingen REM die selbstzerstörerischen Kräfte unseres Planeten und eine überforderte und desillusionierte Weltbevölkerung.

Unter Berücksichtigung der Entstehungshintergründe des Liedes hat es sich als sinnvoll erwiesen, eine vorbereitende Hausaufgabe zu erteilen:

> Watch today's evening news and flip through different channels. Take note of the headlines and pictures that catch your eye/you notice while watching. Do not try to grasp every detail of the coverage. Write down what you remember.

Auf die vorbereitete Hausaufgabe greifen Sie erst am Ende der Bearbeitung zurück. Nach dem ersten Hören sollen die Schülerinnen und Schüler die Musik des Titels zunächst charakterisieren (z. B. mit Begriffen wie *fast tunes, speak-singing, guitar strings, loud, aggressive)* und sich anschließend mit dessen Inhalt auseinandersetzen. Ziel ist es, dass die Schülerinnen und Schüler obige Analyse ansatzweise selbst leisten. Dazu könnten Sie folgenden Arbeitsauftrag geben:

> In a radio interview, Michael Stipe, REM's lead singer, explains the genesis of the song as follows: "I was at Lester Bang's birthday party and I was the only person there whose initials weren't LB. [...] So there was Lenny Bruce, Leonid Breshnev, Leonard Bernstein .... So that ended up in the song along with a lot of stuff I'd seen when I was flipping TV channels [...]"[1]
> Read through the lyrics and try to make a list of the different images from TV news programs Stipe might have encountered while flipping between channels. What concerns are raised in the song? How does the singer respond to them?

Selbstverständlich kommt es an dieser Stelle nicht auf Vollständigkeit an, vielmehr sind gerade die inhaltlichen Widersprüchlichkeiten interessant und das besondere Merkmal dieser Form der Gesellschaftskritik. Eine vollständige plausible Zusammenfassung kann unmöglich geliefert werden und widerspricht auch der Autorenintention. Vielmehr sollten Sie die Kursteilnehmerinnen und -teilnehmer auffordern, Fragen an das Lied zu stellen. Hierbei ergeben sich interessante Diskussionen um mögliche Deutungsversuche. Denkbar ist auch ein fiktives Interview mit Michael Stipe. So können die Schülerinnen und Schüler ihre eigenen Deutungen erläutern.

---

1 Craig Rosen, REM: *Inside Out*, Carlton Books LTD 1997, 2005, ISBN: 184442 449 9, S. 83

Images/concerns	Responses
• the world has its own dynamics (incl. natural disasters as well as man-made conflicts), there is no way anybody can stop this (ll. 1–5) • corrupt governments, war zones, battle fields (ll. 7 ff.) • foreign powers, danger of hostile regimes invading (ll. 8 f.) • illegal migration, overpopulation (l. 12) • military operations elsewhere, escalation of conflicts, proxy wars and crimes related to war, soldiers in combat (ll. 21 ff.) • lies, conspiracies, reluctance to consider peace negotiations (l. 27) • north-south divide, increase of poverty (l. 12)	• you must also serve your own needs, nobody else will do it for you (l. 13) • there is compassion but also alienation and detachment (there are different ways of dealing with the images we receive every day) (ll. 14–17) • we are aware of the dangers, have given up and are not really part of what is going on around us (ll. 18 ff.) • stay where you are, stay safe (ll. 21 f.) • focus on the pleasant aspects in life such as birthday parties as one way of escaping the images presented in the news (ll. 36 f.)

Im anschließenden Unterrichtsgespräch sollten Sie noch auf das Verhältnis von Form und Inhalt und die Schwierigkeiten bei der Analyse eingehen:

1. What do the lyrics remind of you?
2. Why is it so hard to make any sense of the song?

1. a speech contest, a public debate, poetry slam, rap
2. The use of stylistic devices such as comic relief, antithesis, irony; the song is packed with contradictory images.

Zum Abschluss empfiehlt sich folgendes produktionsorientiertes Herangehen: Die Kursteilnehmerinnen und -teilnehmer tauschen ihre Mitschriften aus der Hausaufgabe aus und verfassen auf dieser Grundlage einen eigenen inneren Monolog. Folgender Impuls könnte gegeben werden:

Swap your headline-notes with somebody in the class and compose your own text by arranging the notes in a suitable order and using the artistic form employed by REM.

5.2 Thou art past the tyrant's stroke: William Shakespeare, *Fear No More the Heat o' the Sun*

Wahrscheinlich fragen Sie sich – nicht ohne Berechtigung –, warum dieses Gedicht von Shakespeare in einem Kapitel zusammen mit zeitgenössischen Popsongs auftaucht. Die sprachlichen Unterschiede könnten größer kaum sein. Und auch historisch würde der vorliegende Text aus *Cymbeline* natürlich viel besser in das dritte Kapitel dieser Ausgabe passen. Wir haben das Gedicht aus folgenden Gründen ans Ende der Textsammlung gestellt:

- Nach den vielen anspruchsvollen Texten in den Kapiteln I. bis IV. wollten wir die Sammlung nicht mit vergleichsweise profanen Popsongs enden lassen.
- Inhaltlich wird ein völlig neuer Aspekt thematisiert, der unseres Erachtens nicht ins literaturhistorisch eigentlich besser passende dritte Kapitel gehört.
- Ein ruhiger, nachdenklicher, aber auf seine Weise auch mit einer positiven Aussage verbundener Ausklang schien uns angemessen.

Falls Sie einen Grundkurs unterrichten, wird dies vielleicht die einzige Gelegenheit sein, Ihre Schülerinnen und Schüler an einen Shakespeare-Text heranzuführen und ihnen die einzigartige Schönheit der Sprache zu vermitteln. Da dieses Gedicht verhältnismäßig einfach ist, kann es helfen, den Kursteilnehmerinnen und Kursteilnehmern die Angst vor Texten des Barden zu nehmen.
Sollten Sie über eine Tonaufnahme verfügen[1], spielen Sie diese zunächst ein- oder zweimal vor. Nach Klärung sprachlicher Schwierigkeiten sollte der Text anschließend von den Schülerinnen und Schülern ebenfalls laut gelesen werden, damit diese ein Gefühl für die Rhythmik Shakespeare'scher Lyrik bekommen. (Geben Sie dem Kurs vorher den Hinweis, dass der Akzent über dem zweiten Wort in der letzten Zeile andeutet, dass diese Silbe voll gesprochen wird – „renowned" hat also drei Silben). Auch gegen ein abschließendes Auswendiglernen, ggf. auf freiwilliger Basis, ist unserer Meinung nach nichts einzuwenden.
Mindestens genauso wichtig ist aber natürlich der Inhalt des Gedichtes. Dieser erschließt sich – wie so oft bei Shakespeare – auch über die von ihm verwendeten sprachlichen Mittel.[2]
So bestimmt die Anapher „Fear no more" zu Beginn der ersten drei Strophen eindeutig den Tonfall des Gedichtes, während die Epipher „thee" betont, um wen es geht.

Wir empfehlen, die Schülerinnen und Schüler die folgenden Fragen in Gruppen- oder Partnerarbeit beantworten zu lassen:

1. In your own words, what is the theme of this poem (which is actually part of a play and spoken by two characters)? What is its message?
2. Characterize the atmosphere Shakespeare creates. How does he achieve this?
3. Does he make use of any utopian ideas?
4. What is the effect of the shift in metre in the final stanza?
5. Name other stylistic or rhetorical devices Shakespeare uses in this extract and explain their function.

1. Theme: the significance of succumbing to one's death, which one should not fight, since it is inevitable for all of humanity; once one is

[1] z. B. *Cymbeline – Arkangel Complete* Shakespeare, 2004, Hörkassette, ISBN 1932219471
[2] eine gute Gelegenheit, stilistische Mittel einzuführen oder zu wiederholen (siehe Aufgabe 5.)

dead, one can no longer enjoy the happiness ("joy") or the distress ("moan") that we are allowed to experience during a lifetime; therefore, we should take advantage of the time we have left – Shakespeare's version of Horace's "Carpe Diem".

2. Calm, peaceful; death is shown as an almost welcome alternative to life, which here is mostly described as something threatening, e.g. "winter's rages", "the frown o' the great", "the tyrant's stroke", "the all-dreaded thunder-stone", "witchcraft", "ghost unlaid"; stylistic means: e.g. repetitions (anaphora and epiphora).

3. Such a peaceful environment, which is also called "home" in l. 4, can only be found in death. It is noteworthy that there is no outlook on a "hereafter", i.e. no indication of a life after death, as we found in the first two texts of this collection.

4. Instead of the *iambic pentameter* (five metrical feet per line with alternating stressed and unstressed syllables), which is normally found in Shakespearean plays, the first three stanzas are written in *tetrameter* (four metrical feet per line). The lines of the fourth stanza are even shorter because here the Bard makes use of *trimeter* (three metrical feet per line), obviously to give more urgency to the commands and conjurations in the final lines of the poem. Every evil or harmful creature is to leave the corpse alone so that it will be able to rest in peace for all eternity.

5. anaphora (ll. 1, 7, 13); epiphora (ll. 6, 12, 18, 19–22); personification (l. 2); metaphor (l. 4); masculine rhyme (ll. 1/3, 11/12); feminine rhyme (ll. 2/4); eye-rhyme (ll. 7/9, 23/24); metre, enjambment (ll. 17/18)

Weitere Informationen zur Interpretation des Gedichtes finden Sie hier:
http://wowessays.com/dbase/af3/lva32.shtml

Anhang

a) Die Apokalypse in der Malerei

Neben dem auf Seite 6 der Textausgabe abgebildeten Gemälde von Bosch eignen sich auch die folgenden Bilder u. E. gut zur Diskussion utopischer und/oder dystopischer Aspekte.

Albrecht Dürer: ***Die apokalyptischen Reiter***
http://de.wikipedia.org/wiki/Die_Apokalyptischen_Reiter

Lucas Cranach: ***Die Babylonische Hure***
http://www.conncoll.edu/academics/departments/relstudies/290/theory/revelations/whore.html

Arnold Böcklin: ***Der Krieg***
www.onlinekunst.de/frieden/eingang_d.html

Ludwig Meidner: ***Schrecken des Krieges, Apocalyptic Landscape*** **und** ***The City and Me***
www.uweb.ucsb.edu/~huangyingjie/Fall05/Sturman/Illustrations.pdf

Pablo Picasso: ***Guernica***
http://www.mala.bc.ca/~lanes/english/hemngway/picasso/guernica.htm

Francesco Navarro (alias Moebuis): ***Dystopia***
http://homepage.ntlworld.com/gavin.watson30/INTERVIEW_01_MOEBUIS.htm

Timestretch: ***Dystopia***
http://www.timestretch.com/site/desktop_images_1/

Sammy Cucher und Anthony Aziz: ***Genetics and Culture***
http://www.azizcucher.net/1994.php

b) Musterantworten zu den *while-reading questions* in der Textausgabe

Book of Isaiah
What will the relationship between man and animal be like? p. 8

It will be based on friendship and harmony.

In what respect will the living conditions of the Israelites be different after Judgement Day? p. 9

There will be no need to be afraid since God will come to save the Israelites; disabled people will be healed; desert-like countryside will be turned into a green garden with plenty of water and without any dangerous animals.

The Qur'an
What will life after death be like for the righteous? p. 9

They will live in gardens full of rivers, with "pure and holy" (l. 6) companions, fresh water, milk, wine and fruit.

What will be offered to the righteous in Paradise? p. 10

Alcoholic drinks, which will not make them drunk or cause hangovers; fruit, poultry.

What kind of "Companions" will they have? p. 11

Beautiful virgins of their own age.

What will life be like for sinners?

They will have to suffer in fire or boiling water without any pleasure or refreshment.

Plato: *The Republic I*
According to Plato, what is the ultimate aim of "kallipolis"? p. 13

The happiness of the whole community.

Why is too much happiness of the "guardians" particularly harmful?

The "guardians" are so influential that their corruption might destroy the whole state.

What is the ideal amount of personal happiness? p. 13

Every citizen should be provided with his/her share of happiness.

Why should wealth and poverty be avoided in "kallipolis"?

Both will ultimately lead to unrest and revolution.

Plato: *The Republic II*
What, according to Plato, is a sacred marriage? p. 14

A marriage which the community benefits from most.

p. 15

Why should some men and women have sex often, others rarely?

The more children are born to the "best" partners and the fewer children are born to "inferior" partners, the better.

What is the ultimate aim of marriages?

The number of males should be constant.

What is supposed to happen to the "offspring" of each group? Why?

The children of "good" parents will be taken away from them and reared by the state. The children of "inferior" parents and others born handicapped will be killed.

More: *Utopia*

p. 16

Why are the marriage rules so strict?

→ p. 16/17

Sex is supposed to be a reward for married partners only (for enduring many inconveniences).

How are spouses chosen? Why does the narrator consider this method, on the one hand, ridiculous, yet on the other hand reasonable and even wise?

Spouses are presented in the nude so that "contagious" or "loathsome " (p. 17, l. 10) parts of the bodies cannot be hidden. Europeans might laugh at that or consider it indecent, but as the body "adds not a little to the mind" (p. 17, ll. 12f.), this is a way to be on the safe side.

p. 17

Under which circumstances and regulations are divorces possible?

Only in cases of adultery and "perverseness". Then the "injured" person may marry again, the guilty one not.

When would divorces never be allowed by the authorities?

In cases of old age and/or disease.

Campanella: *The City of The Sun*

p. 18

What is the ultimate purpose of having sex in the City of the Sun?

The "production" of healthy offspring.

According to what criteria are young people "matched"?

The size of sexual organs, height (tall girls matched with tall young men), weight (fat girls matched with slim men and vice versa to avoid similar extremes in their offspring).

p. 19

What are women not allowed to do? Why?

They are not allowed to use cosmetics and/or wear high heels because there is no need for such deception.

Why – according to the Genoese captain – do women outside the City of the Sun apply make-up and wear high-heeled shoes? Which possible consequences of such habits are mentioned?

They do so because of their laziness and inactivity. They will ruin their health and that of their children.

p. 20

Which role does love play in this society?

Flirting and other forms of platonic love are allowed; sexual intercourse though is only permitted to selected partners.

Swift: *Gulliver's Travels*

p. 21

Why should parents "not be trusted with the education of their own children"?

Their parents didn't do them a favour when bringing them into the world, neither did they consider their upbringing during their lovemaking.

What are visiting parents not allowed to do?

They are not allowed to give their children presents or show any tenderness with the exception of two quick kisses.

p. 22

What is the only difference between the education of girls and boys?

The females' exercises are less strenuous. They learn about domestic life, and their general curriculum is smaller than that of the boys.

Which reason is given for the differentiation?

A married wife is to be "reasonable and agreeable"; in other words, she is not supposed to contradict her (better-educated) husband.

Wells: *The Time Machine*

p. 25

What does he consider to be the ultimate consequence of the social efforts of his contemporaries?

The whole world will improve to an amazing extent (no more diseases, annoying insects or fungi, but instead peaceful people in perfect health, living in wonderful places, wearing fine clothes without having to work for their livelihood, surrounded by beautiful plants and animals in abundance).

p. 26

Why does he initially consider this world of the future a "social paradise"?

No more commerce, struggle, competition, but instead mutual understanding.

Who – according to the Time Traveller – might have been the ancestors of the Eloi, who those of the Morlocks?

Eloi: the former "Upper-world people" (p. 26, ll. 21 f.), the aristocracy – or ruling class – of the Time Traveller's own time.
Morlocks: the former working class.

p. 27

What is the major nourishment of the subterranean people?

The Eloi, who he here calls "mere fatted cattle" (p. 27, ll. 42f.).

Huxley: *Brave New World*

p. 30

What is the first difference mentioned between Alphas and Betas on the one hand, and Gammas, Deltas and Epsilons on the other?

Alphas and Betas are left in their bottles, whereas Gammas, Deltas and Epsilons have to undergo "Bokanovsky's Process".

What is the advantage of "bokanovskification"?

Up to ninety-six identical human beings develop from one fertilized egg.

p. 35

How are Epsilons "produced"?

Their brains are partly destroyed through a reduction of oxygen.

p. 36

What is the aim of "Heat conditioning"?

The embryos undergoing it will later, as grown-up men and women, love to live in a hot, tropical climate.

What is the secret of happiness in the Brave New World?

Everybody is predestined, i.e. conditioned while still in a test tube, to live happily, no matter where or under which circumstances.

Orwell: *1984*

p. 39

What are the two functions of the "telescreen"?

It is a means of propaganda and surveillance at the same time.

Atwood: *The Handmaid's Tale*

p. 41

Characterize the narrator from these opening lines.

Insecure, self-conscious, somehow unhappy with her present situation, missing her friend Moira, who would know what to do, suicidal (?)

p. 44

Name the successive steps which were taken to turn a Western democracy into a religious dictatorship. [...]

The President and the members of Congress were killed; military commanders took over power and declared a state of emergency, blaming Islamic fanatics; the Constitution was suspended, the press censored or silenced; in-town visas became obligatory; sex-shops, brothels etc. were closed down.
The narrator herself was "stunned" (p. 44, l. 6), but like most people seemed to agree to most measures, considering them adequate for safety or moral reasons ("everyone was [stunned]" p. 44, l. 7; "Everyone approved" p. 44, l. 24; "We all knew" p. 44, l. 30). Hardly anybody seemed to oppose the coup actively; they instead pinned their hopes on vague promises of "new elections" (p. 44, ll. 25f.).

The narrator has a very different personality from her friend Moira, especially when facing conflict. Describe these differences.

p. 47

The narrator seems helpless, stunned, unable to cope with the situation and totally dependent on her husband. Moira is better informed, far more energetic and determined. She tries to explain the situation to the narrator.

What role did the confiscation and transfer of property play in the shift of power between the female narrator and her husband Luke, and why?

p. 48

A new patriarchal society had come into existence. Women were now totally dependent on their husbands. Luke was understanding and comforting, yet the narrator felt patronized by him.

The narrator not only has a very different personality from her friend Moira, but also from her mother. Give examples.

p. 49

Her mother: Alternative lifestyle; "ever-changing circle of friends" (p. 49, l. 36); politically-active feminist, who frequently went to violent demonstrations (pro-abortion, anti-pornography), willing to fight policemen.

Characterize the images used in this passage. What does Nick signify for the narrator?

p. 50

"like oyster spawn from the sea" (l. 32): simile, somehow aiming at the reader's sense of smell. Nick inhales the smelly air. In connection with words like "pollen", "pulpy growth", "prodigal breeding" (p. 50, ll. 31 f.) sexual undertones are included. The narrator feels attracted to him despite herself. "like a cat's back arching" (l. 34): simile. In the context of words and expression like "muscles", "bare", "shamelessly", "Where does the tan end?" (p. 50, ll. 33–36), the reader once more gets the impression that the narrator is sexually aroused by Nick.
"He's only my flag, my semaphore." (ll. 37 f.): metaphor. On the one hand, she considers him to be a – sexually attractive – spy, on the other, he seems to give her secret signals by the way his cap is set.

Sum up to what extent the relationship between the married couple has changed.

p. 51

She does not want to have sex with him, feels frigid and indifferent. She is aware that everything that used to be theirs is now just his. She even thinks that she now belongs to him, instead of the two of them belonging to each other. She feels shrunken, seems to have lost all self-confidence and believes that Luke does not care about this.

L. and A. Wachowski: *The Matrix*

Why is Neo being interrogated by Agent Smith? By what means does he try to make Neo confess?

p. 52

Neo is supposed to be a notorious hacker. Means used: threats, the offer of a deal (the agents want him to help them to find Morpheus), weird means of torture and surveillance.

p. 54 Who is Morpheus? Why does he contact Neo?

He is the leader of an underground movement and contacts Neo, because he believes him to be the chosen "One" (p. 54, l. 20), who alone will be able to rescue and liberate mankind from slavery.

p. 57 Explain the symbolic meaning of the blue and the red pill.

Taking the blue pill symbolizes living a life without taking risks. After taking it, Neo would further be blinded "from the truth" (p. 56, l. 39) and live in a "dreamworld" (p. 61, l. 20). The red pill symbolizes the opposite: Life will certainly be less comfortable for Neo, but he will broaden his horizon and discover what life really is like.

p. 60 Sum up Neo's experience in the Power Plant.

He sees himself as he has really lived – or rather vegetated – up to that moment: He has been nothing more than a power supplier for machines, which have sucked energy out of him through tubes and IVs. He watched a countless number of human beings who are in the same predicament without really knowing about this. After he unsuccessfully tries to free himself, an insect-like machine arrives and rescues him.

p. 61 What seems to have happened to the world between the end of the twentieth century and Neo's time?

Obviously, a man-made global catastrophe has taken place and utterly destroyed our planet. Intelligent Machines have enslaved people to exploit human energy like that of batteries.

Atwood: *Oryx and Crake I*

p. 64 What does Jimmy, the protagonist of the novel, blame Crake for?

Jimmy is all alone, probably the last human being alive after a world-wide catastrophe initiated by Crake.

What might be the function of the disinfectant?

The disinfectant is to prevent the further spread of a livestock disease.

p. 65 Why was this "bonfire" made?

The so-called "bonfire" is to burn the corpses of an enormous number of cows, sheep and pigs, which have obviously died of the contagious disease.

p. 66 What is suspected by the two grown-ups?

They suspect that the disease was brought in on purpose to create a lack of meat and raise the prices.

Atwood: *Oryx and Crake II*

What is Crake's lifework?

Nothing less than the creation of a new human species, the Crakers

Who are the "Crakers"? p. 67

They are beautiful, artificially-created herbivores of different colors, almost immune to diseases, with a UV-resistant skin, gentle, naive, and unable to be violent or jealous; all in all, far better adjusted to the new post-apocalyptic world than Jimmy.

What advantages over "normal" people are the "Crakers" supposed to have? p. 69

(See answer to the previous question.)

Anderson: *Feed*

How are schools of the past portrayed in contrast to School™? p. 70

According to Titus, school was run by the government (which he compares to the Nazis) and full of guns, drugs and teachers, who were pimps. Lessons were boring, the curriculum irrelevant. In contrast, School™ teaches the students that big corporations are taking care of the students and America's future. They learn about new technology, shopping bargains and the latest fashion.

In what ways do the narrator Titus and his girlfriend Violet differ from each other? p. 71

Violet's parents were poor and could not afford to buy her a Feed when she was little, plus they did not want her to have one. Since she did not get hers until she was seven, she is far smarter and a more independent thinker than Titus. She is interested in ecological and political affairs, and is critical of the US' involvement in South America.

How are their differences reflected in their style of speech?

Titus: unable to communicate about sophisticated matters ("da da da" e.g. p. 70, ll. 10f.), imprecise, very limited vocabulary, slang, simple sentences, faulty grammar
Violet: Although we only get to know her statements indirectly through Titus' limited vocabulary and grammar, it becomes obvious that she is pondering about serious matters and able to talk about them. Words, expressions and thoughts like "two-party-system" (p. 71, l. 39), "both parties are in the pocket of big business" (p. 71, ll. 40f.), the difference between a "republic" and a "democracy" (p. 71, ll. 12–20) definitely come from her not Titus.

How do his parents first try to console him? p. 74

First they assure him of their affection and tell him that he looks just the way they wanted him to.

What is their second, more successful attempt like? p. 75

Then they try to cheer him up by giving him an expensive present.

Sheckley: *The Perfect Woman*

What seems to be wrong with Myra? p. 77

She answers her husband's questions too slowly.

Zager and Evans: *In the Year 2525*

p. 79

Name three technological inventions and their consequences as envisioned in this song.

Pills dominate people's lives; their arms and legs have become limp since they are not needed anymore because machines do everything for people; children are taken from glass tubes.

p. 80

Explain "He's taken everything this old Earth can give. And he ain't put back nothing."

Man has exploited all the Earth's natural resources but has done nothing to improve living conditions on our planet.

The Police: *Walking in Your Footsteps*

p. 81

Why are humans and dinosaurs compared in this song?

The mighty dinosaurs ruled the world and disappeared. The same might happen to mankind if we don't learn from their example.

p. 82

Why is line 14 also a warning for the future of the human race?

We also consider ourselves invincible.

Who are "they"?

Probably people of the future.

Explain the relevance of "The meek shall inherit the earth" with regard to this song.

If people are not "meek", i.e. neither humble nor patient, they will have no future on this planet.

Faithless: *Mass Destruction*

p. 86

Which weapons of mass destruction does the songwriter name?

"A wicked mind" (p. 86, l. 2), "Misinformation" (p. 86, l. 4), "Racism" (p. 86, l. 7), "Fear" (p. 86, l. 8), "Greed" (p. 87, l. 28), "Inaction" (p. 87, l. 30)

p. 87

Where does the father have to go?

He is probably a soldier, who has to go to war.

EINFACH ENGLISCH

Edited by Hans Kröger

American Beauty
87 S., Best.-Nr. 041225

Margaret Atwood: The Handmaid's Tale
73 S., Best.-Nr. 041208

Paul Auster: Moon Palace
76 S., Best.-Nr. 041226

Mark Behr: The Smell of Apples
77 S., Best.-Nr. 041215

Bend it Like Beckham
88 S., Best.-Nr. 041212

T. C. Boyle: The Tortilla Curtain
75 S., Best.-Nr. 041203

Ray Bradbury: Fahrenheit 451
72 S., Best.-Nr. 041214

Criminals & Detectives
96 S., Best.-Nr. 041207
Textausgabe, 98 S., Best.-Nr. 041206

Cultures in Conflict? – Literature on Ethnic Relationships
114 S., Best.-Nr. 041220
Textausgabe, 148 S., Best.-Nr. 041218
Audio-CD, Best.-Nr. 062407

Dead Poets Society
67 S., Best.-Nr. 041255

East is East
ca. 96 S., Best.-Nr. 041228

Echoes of the Empire – The Mixed Voices of a Colonial Past; 20th Century English Short Stories
120 S., Best.-Nr. 041223
Textausgabe, 168 S., Best.-Nr. 041224
Audio-CD, 78 min., Best.-Nr. 062405

Forrest Gump
65 S., Best.-Nr. 041231

William Golding: Lord of the Flies
98 S., Best.-Nr. 041217

Mark Haddon: The Curious Incident of the Dog in the Night-Time
90 S., Best.-Nr. 041252

Lorraine Hansberry: A Raisin in the Sun
98 S., Best.-Nr. 041241

Nick Hornby: About a Boy
93 S., Best.-Nr. 041245

Aldous Huxley: Brave New World
93 S., Best.-Nr. 041249

Bernard MacLaverty: Cal
71 S., Best.-Nr. 041239

Arthur Miller: The Crucible
84 S., Best.-Nr. 041209

Monty Python
71 S., Best.-Nr. 041221

Joyce Carol Oates: Big Mouth & Ugly Girl
84 S., Best.-Nr. 041233

George Orwell: Animal Farm
80 S., Best.-Nr. 041257
Textausgabe, 88 S., Best.-Nr. 041258

Poetry
103 S., Best.-Nr. 041227

Roman Polanski: Macbeth
103 S., Best.-Nr. 041235

Political Speeches – Historical & Topical Issues
ca. 130 S., Best.-Nr. 041236
Textausgabe, 132 S., Best.-Nr. 041234
Audio-CD, Best.-Nr. 062409

Ruth Prawer Jhabvala: Heat and Dust
88 S., Best.-Nr. 041199

J. B. Priestley: An Inspector Calls
64 S., Best.-Nr. 041201
Textausgabe, 80 S., Best.-Nr. 041200

Rabbit-Proof Fence
54 S., Best.-Nr. 041240

Sam Shepard: True West
65 S., Best.-Nr. 041210

Thunderheart – Exploring Native America
112 S., Best.-Nr. 041211

Utopia and Dystopia – Exploring Alternative Worlds
92 S., Best.-Nr. 041204
Textausgabe, 90 S., Best.-Nr. 041202

Charles Webb: The Graduate
60 S., Best.-Nr. 041205

Fordern Sie unseren Prospekt zur Reihe an:
Informationen zum Nulltarif ✆ 08 00 / 1 81 87 87

SCHÖNINGH VERLAG
Postfach 2540 · 33055 Paderborn

Schöningh

E-Mail: info@schoeningh.de
Internet: www.schoeningh-schulbuch.de